A study of services for

Multiple Sc

Lessons for manag

d

ROYAL COLLEGE OF PHYSICIANS

Acknowledgements

This project was funded by the Department of Health through the Royal College of Physicians Research Unit (now the Clinical Effectiveness and Evaluation Unit), and we are grateful for their financial and practical support. We acknowledge the enthusiastic co-operation of all the patients who participated in the formal audit, and the countless other patients who contributed ideas and support.

We thank all the individual professional staff from health, social services and other organisations, and the GPs for their time and support. The local Multiple Sclerosis Society and the Association for Research in Multiple Sclerosis both gave invaluable help. The Multiple Sclerosis Research Charity gave financial support. Dr Alan Thompson chaired an early meeting and last, but by no means least, Miss Tracey Wing gave unstintingly of her time and enthusiasm in answering the phone, developing databases, writing letters, developing forms, etc. Thank you to everyone, especially to those we have omitted.

DTW
QG

Royal College of Physicians of London
11 St Andrews Place, London NW1 4LE

Registered Charity No 210508

Copyright © 2001 Royal College of Physicians of London

ISBN 1 86016 148 0

Designed and typeset by the Publications Unit of the Royal College of Physicians

Printed in Great Britain by The Chameleon Press Limited, London

Preface

Specialisation led to great increases in industrial efficiency in the 19th and 20th centuries. People, teams and organisations became increasingly good at doing some limited task. Complex processes were broken down into a series of simple tasks, and individual people or groups undertook specified activities that together completed the process. Health services followed this trend, with increasing specialisation and diversity of professions and specialties. However, services that focus on one health problem such as gastrointestinal bleeding or breast cancer treatment will inevitably not be so good at managing other health problems. This report investigates how patients with complex problems fare in a specialised health service.

In the last few decades the health service has had to manage more patients with multiple problems and with problems that persist. Elderly patients form one group, and geriatric medicine developed in response to the need for a service able to diagnose and manage patients with multiple pathology (although increasingly it focuses on the acute medical aspects of the elderly). More recently, it has become obvious that other groups of patients have long-term complex health problems. Examples include children with congenital or neonatally-acquired damage and disease, patients with diabetes, and patients with neurological disability arising from many different causes in childhood or as adults.

Some patients with complex long-term problems are managed within services that specialise to a greater or lesser extent. Currently four generic specialist services (paediatric, geriatric, mental health, learning disability) take some responsibility for all the health care needs of their defined populations. There are also some single specialist services (palliative care, oncology) that take on some long-term responsibility, but there are other groups of patients with long-term needs that are not met, the most obvious example being patients with neurological disability. In response to this need, specialist services focused on the management of long-term disability are beginning to emerge in Britain, although they have existed in other European countries for decades. Most newly developed services grow in an unplanned way but, because this country has few specialist disability services at present, there is an opportunity to develop services that could reflect and meet the needs of patients in a way that is efficient, effective and equitable.

This report discusses two major topics relating to services for patients with long-term and complex health needs:

i   Clinical governance.
ii Service organisation.

It considers these topics at the level of the whole population of a large area such as that of a health authority. It outlines how the quality of services for patients with long-term complex health problems might be monitored and improved, and suggests a framework for organising services.

The aim of clinical governance is the efficient delivery of effective services. This requires that organisations, both large and small, have ways of assessing the quality of the services for which they are responsible. Most health care needs are met by primary care services, but patients with less common problems, whether they are to do with diagnosis or management, need specialist services that serve larger populations. Health authorities are charged with ensuring that the whole population receives the health services that fulfil their needs. They will have special responsibility for patients or services that straddle boundaries, where there is a risk that no one will own the problem or monitor quality. This report investigates how quality can be monitored and improved for the many patients with chronic diseases whose specialist needs span different service providers and extend over many years.

Patients with multiple sclerosis (MS) might be considered a paradigm for all patients with long-term complex disability who do not easily fall within the remit of any one organisation:

- They will often call upon a wide variety of services both within and outside the health services.
- Their needs do not readily fall within the remit of any one organisation.
- They are usually older than 16 years and so not the responsibility of paediatric services, but younger than 65 years (or 75 years) and so not the responsibility of geriatric services.
- They do not have a mental health problem or learning disability, and so fall outside the other two major generic services.

Consequently, it is possible that this group of younger patients with severe disability receive poor services.

At the same time, it is now known that patients with relatively rare complex problems generally have better outcomes if managed by specialist services. This specifically applies to complex disability, as evidenced by the meta-analysis of stroke unit services[1] which found that a multi-disciplinary, co-ordinated specialist stroke service undoubtedly delivers a better outcome, probably at little extra cost. There are, however, currently few specialist neurological disability services.

In 1995, a project was set up to develop a way for evaluating the quality of services delivered to patients with MS, with the hope that a method to improve services would be devised that could be widely used in other conditions such as chronic obstructive airways disease. This project was initiated by the late Dr Anthony Hopkins, modelled at least in part upon the successful programme that developed the Stroke Audit Package which has now been extended to form a national audit. It was anticipated that this project would be the first step in devising a similar audit package for heath authorities interested in evaluating services for patients with MS. Unfortunately, Dr Hopkins did not live to see the product of his enthusiasm, but we believe that his goal has been achieved.

Two main messages arise from this project:

i Patients with MS present to statutory services, primarily health and social services, with a wide variety of ill-defined problems at various levels: new or troublesome symptoms, difficulties with a wide variety of daily activities such as mobility or work, problems with housing, social isolation, etc. Each patient has a different mixture.

ii Services are not organised around the patient, but around a bewildering variety of specific problems. Further, they are located in different places run by different organisations, few of which have any specific expertise in MS.

Two consequences follow:

i   It is effectively impossible to audit the quality of services for this group of patients.

ii A framework is needed to help patients and service providers understand and organise the patchwork of services so that each patient's needs can be identified and met.

This report describes the audit project in some detail, and should help anyone interested in developing similar projects. We travelled down several blind alleys which it is hoped others may now avoid, and developed methods which we hope others will improve. The methods described are not perfect nor are the data epidemiologically perfect, but we hope the project has provided useful information and some insight into ways of improving service quality.

This report also develops a framework which should help in the development of a coherent and comprehensive network of services for patients with chronic disease and disability. The framework is based on the World Health Organization's model that underlies the International Classification of Impairments, Disabilities and Handicaps.

Finally, based on our experience and the data collected, the report makes recommendations on how services for patients with long-term health problems can be audited and organised. We hope that this project will help improve services for the significant and increasing number of patients who are not acutely ill but who need, at least intermittently, help from health and social services.

Derick Wade

Quentine Green

Oxford

Reference

1   Stroke Unit Trialists' Collaboration. Collaborative systematic review of the randomised trials of organised inpatient (stroke unit) care after stroke. *Br Med J* 1997;**314**:1151–9.

Contents

Summary and recommendations

Recent reports on service provision for people with multiple sclerosis (MS) suggest that services addressing the needs of this group of people fall short of expectations. This project aimed to develop a method which any health authority could use to audit and improve local services. The objectives were to develop simple, practical methods to determine:

▓ how well services in a health authority area met the needs of people with MS;

▓ which services consistently failed to meet those needs;

▓ how they failed; and

▓ the actions needed to remedy deficiencies effectively.

The wider aim of the audit was to learn whether – and how – the results obtained might be applied more generally to other chronic disability. The solving, or otherwise, of many of the problems experienced with MS should have lessons for other disabilities.

The initial phase aimed to identify specific issues raised by users, providers and purchasers of the various services. Specialists from other areas were also consulted. This pilot study confirmed that most people and organisations agreed that there were problems in identifying and meeting the needs of people with MS. Further preliminary work was carried out to establish practical methods of audit, and to establish baseline data against which any results could be compared. This involved:

▓ setting up a register of people with MS willing to participate;

▓ estimating and confirming the size of the problem through a census of general practitioners (GPs);

▓ developing a postal questionnaire to characterise the clinical status and problems experienced by patients;

▓ using this questionnaire to estimate the frequency of certain problems; and

▓ specifically addressing problems arising in the process of making a new diagnosis of MS.

In addition, strategies were developed to overcome possible problems during the audit, including devising methods to validate data collected.

The main audit study was carried out over 10 months and was based on new or worsening MS related problems. It involved 226 people who carried audit cards on which they recorded what services and individual professional staff they came in contact with, how often, what for and what was done. Because of delays in learning about new contacts, patients were asked to report new problems by telephone. Prospective telephone checks were also made at intervals to check if any new problems had arisen. All contacts were recorded, and analysis revealed those aspects of services that were causing difficulty in meeting people's needs. The areas in which data were collected included:

▓ the presenting (new) symptom or problem;

▓ those health professionals/services contacted;

▓ any problems with referrals (NHS or social services);

▓ other problems with social services;

- equipment supply (including waiting times);
- benefits supplied;
- investigations required and waiting times (including for magnetic resonance imaging);
- any treatments required; and
- any problems with the audit technique.

The data collected vividly demonstrated the great variety of problems experienced and services used. Over the 10-month audit period more than 284 new problems arose in 112 of the 226 patients who participated (although only 180 remained in full contact with the study). The following *new* problems were reported: mobility (58 people), urinary symptoms (39), 'general deterioration' (30), gastrointestinal problems (26), significant pain (24) and injuries due to falls (15). A wide variety of other new problems were experienced by between three and thirteen people per problem.

New advice was wanted by 25 people, 31 different professional groups or services were contacted and, in addition, 15 different specialist hospital consultant services were used. These services spanned many different locations and organisations. Patients with MS never formed the sole or main focus of any service, and were usually a minor group within each service.

Many individual difficulties were noted. For example:
- three patients developed pressure sores while in hospital;
- there were delays in providing equipment;
- some problems recurred and others were not resolved within the time of the study; and
- some patients' problems were not recognised or acknowledged by services until the auditor took action.

The process of making and giving the diagnosis was studied using a semi-structured interview to elicit information about the patients' experiences. Fifteen volunteers were recruited for interview. The resulting data were subjected to content analysis to identify common themes relating to problems experienced. The main finding was that most patients were not very satisfied with the process of telling the diagnosis, and this dissatisfaction was mainly attributable to the perceived attitude of the doctors concerned.

Recommendations

The main recommendations are:

i   Auditing of disability services is best approached using individual patients as 'probes';

ii   Patients with MS could be used to study disability services generally;

iii   Health authorities might improve services for people with MS through developing specialist disability services for patients with neurological diseases, and then appointing a person with special knowledge of MS to act as a 'point of reference'. This person, who might be from any health profession, would need to be familiar with most aspects of MS and disability, have good knowledge of local services, and would probably best be integrated into the local neurology centre or neurological disability centre;

iv   Randomised controlled trials should be undertaken to evaluate a variety of ways of providing this service.

Part 1

Background to the study

1 Introduction

1.1 Health services are good at diagnosing and treating patients who present with acute illnesses, but a variety of formal and informal reports have suggested that there is scope for improvement in services for patients with disability. For example, a recent audit of stroke services within the UK showed that few patients are managed by specialist stroke unit services despite long-standing evidence of their effectiveness.[1] Patients with acute spinal cord injury are probably the only group of people with long-term disability to be managed by a dedicated specialist service. The benefits are self-evident: life expectancy is now almost normal, and many people with spinal injury work and live independently with few health or other problems. Unfortunately, no other significant group of disabled people receives such a good service, although there are many more people disabled by other diseases. This chapter briefly sets the scene for the report and study undertaken.

Disability services

1.2 Patients with disability receive suboptimal services for a variety of reasons. Until the last few decades there were relatively few young disabled patients. In Britain, the specialty of rehabilitation was recognised only in 1986, and disability is still scarcely taught in most medical schools. The public perception, actually untrue, is that there is little research in the field of disability and that outcomes are difficult to measure. Services for acute life-threatening illnesses gain a higher political priority.

1.3 One particular reason for the lack of attention to patients with disability has been the absence of any scientifically credible, agreed framework for understanding and analysing the problems faced by patients. Typically, two models are proposed, both of which are in fact difficult to define. The conflict between them, more apparent than real, does not advance the development of useful services:

i The '*medical model*' focuses on the patient and the disease. It is usually presented by those opposed to the involvement of health professionals, and in fact does not seem to be used by anyone. It is pilloried as 'blaming the patient'.

ii In contrast, the '*social model*' locates the problem with society, almost denying the very existence of disability.

1.4 Over the last two decades the World Health Organization (WHO) has developed a comprehensive model (or framework) that underlies the International Classification of Impairments, Disabilities, and Handicaps, now entering its second version. This framework includes both the medical and social models, and is extremely useful in understanding the nature of disability and rehabilitation services.[2]

1.5 A second major reason why patients with a chronic disease associated with complex disability do not receive good services is because many of them present with problems that do not neatly fall within the remit of any one service, as may be exemplified by a survey of 150 patients with multiple sclerosis (MS) (see Chapter 5). Sometimes a small number of appropriate specific services may be identified, but more commonly the patient will need to use services that span organisational and professional boundaries. Given the frequent significant resource implications of accepting responsibility for such patients, they often have difficulty in finding anyone to take an interest. It is not so much that they fall between the gaps, but rather that they are forced into the holes between the services.

Multiple sclerosis

1.6 Patients with MS are a good exemplar of the difficulties faced. MS, a demyelinating disorder affecting the central nervous system, is the most common cause of severe disability in people between the ages of 20 and 50 years.[3,4] It is varied in its presentation and course. Health systems need to respond appropriately to the often progressive and always unpredictable nature of this disease. Anecdotal reports from patients with MS suggest serious gaps in meeting the needs of patients. The major areas identified include:

- a lack of information;
- poor support during diagnosis;
- a need for ongoing, lifelong assessment in at least some patients; and
- a need for services to be more co-ordinated and tailored to meet individual needs.

The Oxfordshire Multiple Sclerosis Service Audit

1.7 Anecdotes may highlight potential problems in service quality, but more specific information is required to assist individual services gauge their effectiveness and efficiency, because services will vary between health authorities and other factors will differ in different areas. The Oxfordshire Multiple Sclerosis Service Audit was established in collaboration with the late Dr Anthony Hopkins from the Research Unit of the Royal College of Physicians to address this issue. The project was carried out over two years between February 1995 and February 1997.

The aim

1.8 The aim of the audit was to develop a method which could be used by any health authority to audit and improve local services.

The objectives

1.9 The objectives were to develop simple, practical methods suitable for any health authority to determine:

- how well services in their area meet the needs of people with MS;
- which services consistently fail to meet those needs, and how they fail; and
- the action needed to remedy deficiencies effectively.

1.10 The project will be described in later chapters. First, the model derived from that developed by the WHO will be described in outline, and the nature of rehabilitation services described.

2 | Disability and rehabilitation: definitions and a framework

2.1 One major problem facing anyone involved in disability services is the lack of a commonly agreed terminology or framework. Different people interpret almost all terms differently. There is now a growing consensus on a general framework,[2] although it is not universally accepted. This chapter outlines a framework and the terminology used in the remainder of this report.

Models of illness

2.2 A patient can be considered to have an illness when he/she shows one or more of a group of behaviours recognised and acknowledged by society as indicating the presence of disease or damage (injury) in a person (patient). This gives the patient certain privileges (eg to stop work, to access health care), but also confers certain duties (eg to get better).

2.3 There are many models of disability and illness,[5–7] most of which are similar to the World Health Organization's (WHO) model of Impairment, Disabilities (now termed Activities), and Handicaps (now termed Participation),[8,9] usually referred to as the WHO ICIDH model. The original model, published in 1980[10], was recognised as incomplete. Together with the terminology, it has been revised and expanded[9] to draw attention to three aspects of the patient's context:

i   the person's past experiences which may determine his/her attitudes, beliefs and expectations (ie 'internal environment');

ii the person's external environment, including other people as helpers; and

iii the person's social or cultural environment.

2.4 An outline of the model, with definitions of the important terms, is shown in Table 2.1. In essence, it follows a systems analytic approach to illness, and suggests that illness can be considered as a hierarchy of interacting systems with four levels:

i   the organ (eg the nervous system);

ii the whole person;

iii the person's interaction with his/her environment; and

iv the person's position or status within his/her own society.

2.5 These systems or levels of illness are also influenced by three other 'environmental' systems:

i   the person's given internal state;

ii the person's given physical environment; and

iii the person's given social environment.

2.6   The model fails to recognise two important aspects of illness:

■   the person's experience or perception of the illness at each level; and

■   the person's overall response to his/her situation, and perception of his/her 'quality of life'.

2.7   More recent and complex models have incorporated these aspects.[7] A model derived from the ICIDH-2 and Post *et al*[7] (Table 2.2) incorporates both quality of life and the subjective aspects of illness. The expanded model will not be used much in this report. It is, however, relevant when considering services if we want to focus an intervention upon one box, such as the subjective component of personal context where there is evidence that improving self-esteem may lead to health gains.[11] For example, teaching coping skills, which might be considered as affecting personal context, has been shown to benefit patients with multiple sclerosis (MS).[12] These models of illness can be of great practical value in that certain consequences or lessons flow from them.[13]

2.8   This model helps in several ways, not least by defining disability which is often not understood or agreed. The definition used here is that:

disability refers to the activities or behaviours of an individual that are altered in quality or quantity as part of the illness

2.9   In other words, disability refers to activities that the person used to – or wishes to – undertake that are either no longer undertaken, or are performed in a different way from that used prior to the illness or from that expected or wanted by the person concerned.

Table 2.1 Rehabilitation model: the World Health Organization International Classification of Impairments, Disabilities, and Handicaps 2 framework.

Level of illness

Term	Synonym	Definition
Pathology	Disease/diagnosis	Refers to abnormalities or changes in the structure and/or function of an **organ or organ system**
Impairment	Symptoms/signs	Refers to abnormalities or changes in the structure and/or function of the **whole body** set in **personal context**
Activity (was *disability*)	Function/ observed behaviour	Refers to abnormalities, changes or restrictions in the interaction between a person and his/her environment or **physical context** (ie changes in the **quality or quantity** of behaviour)
Participation (was *handicap*)	Social positions/roles	Refers to changes, limitations, or 'abnormalities' in the **position** of the person in their **social context**

Contextual factors

Domain	Examples	Comment
Personal	Previous illness	Primarily refers to **attitudes, beliefs** and **expectations**, often arising from previous experience of illness in self or others, but also to personal characteristics
Physical	House, local shops, carers	Primarily refers to local physical **structures** but also includes people as **carers** (not as social partners)
Social	Laws, friends, family	Primarily refers to **legal** and local **cultural** setting, including expectations of important others

Note: this model is usually prefaced with the words: 'In the context of illness, ...'.

Rehabilitation

2.10 Rehabilitation is also a much misunderstood word. It has three separate facets:

- structure (its characteristics);
- processes; and
- outcomes (aims).

2.11 Some definitions are shown in Box 2.1, where it can be seen that the main difference between rehabilitation and most other health services is that rehabilitation has as its centre of attention the patient's disability (ie the alteration or restriction in activities) rather than the patient's disease (pathology). Figure 2.1 illustrates the process, and Table 2.3 shows some of the interventions that may be needed within rehabilitation, illustrating the range of interventions that may occur in managing someone with a disability.

2.12 One important consequence of this rehabilitation model is that the process of rehabilitation is not restricted to patients with diseases or pathologies where recovery is anticipated.[2]

Table 2.2 Expanded model of illness (the World Health Organization International Classification of Impairments, Disabilities, and Handicaps-2 plus framework): a way of describing an individual's situation.

'Location' of description	Subjective/internal Experience, attributions and beliefs of the patient	Objective/external Observations made, and implications drawn, by others
Level of description (Term used)		
Organ within person: (*pathology*)	**Disease** Label attached by person, usually on basis of belief and experience	**Diagnosis** Label attached by others, usually on basis of investigation
Person: (*impairment*)	**Symptoms** Somatic sensation, experienced moods, thoughts, etc	**Signs** Observable abnormalities (absence or change), often elicited explicitly, and deficits assumed from observations
Person in environment: (*behaviour/'activities'*)	**Perceived ability** What person feels they can and cannot do, and opinion on quality of performance	**Disability/activities** What others note person does do, quantification of that performance (not what others think should be done)
Person in society: (*roles/'participation'*)	**Life satisfaction** Person's judgement or valuation of their own role performance (what and how well)	**Handicap/participation** Judgement or valuation of important others (local culture) on role performance (what and how well)
Context of illness		
Personal context	**'Personality'** Person's attitudes, expectations, beliefs, goals, outlook, reasoning style, etc	**'Past history'** Observed/recorded behaviour prior to and early on in this illness
Physical context	**Personal importance** Person's attitude towards specific people, locations, etc	**Resources** Description of physical (buildings, equipment, etc) and personal (carers, etc) resources available
Social context	**Local culture** People and organisations important to person, and their culture, especially family and people in same accommodation	**Society** The society lived in and the laws, duties and responsibilities expected from and the rights of members of that society
Totality of illness		
Quality of life: summation of effects	**Contentment** Person's assessment of and reaction to achievement or failure of important goals. Or sense of being a worthwhile person.	**Social involvement** Extent of positive interaction with society, contributing to social networks

---

Box 2.1 Rehabilitation: definitions of its three facets (process, structure, outcome)

Process of rehabilitation

Rehabilitation is a reiterative, active, educational, problem-solving process focused on a patient's behaviour (disability) with the following components:

- assessment, the identification of the nature and extent of the patient's problems and the factors relevant to their resolution, including the patient's assets;
- goal setting;
- intervention, which may include either or both of:
  – treatments, which affect the process of change;
  – support (care), which maintains the patient's life and safety;
- evaluation, to check on the effects of any intervention.

Structure: characteristics of a rehabilitation service

The characteristics of a service that specialises in rehabilitation are that it comprises a multidisciplinary group (team) of people who focus their attention on a patient's disability *and*

- work together towards common goals with each patient;
- involve and educate the patient and family in the process;
- have relevant expertise and experience (knowledge and skills); and
- can, between them, resolve most of the common problems faced by their patients.

Outcome: aims of rehabilitation

The three aims of the rehabilitation process are to:

- maximise the participation of the patient in his/her chosen social setting;
- minimise the pain and distress experienced by the patient; and
- minimise the distress of, and stress on, the patient's family and/or carers.

Rehabilitation is applicable to any patient with any disability arising in the context of any illness with any underlying cause. The achievable goals of rehabilitation will vary according to that underlying cause, but in all cases the goals set must also take into account the wishes and expectations of the patient and other interested parties.[14] Equally, the nature of the interventions may vary depending upon the underlying causes. The model also highlights that disability is only weakly linked to diagnosis. This is illustrated in Fig 2.2 which shows some of the links that may exist between disability and the different levels of an illness.

Lessons from this framework

2.13   In the context both of planning services and of monitoring their quality, the theoretical model described above highlights some important points:

i   Realistic goal setting depends upon accurate knowledge of the underlying pathology because this is the primary determinant of prognosis (in a general, not specific sense). Consequently, all services helping disabled people must have input from specialists who can both diagnose the underlying causes and advise on the nature of the disease, the likely associated impairments and the likely future for those patients.

ii   The link between pathology and disability is usually weak. Most pathology (ie most disease processes) will give rise to more than one impairment, and the impairments likely to occur depend upon the pathology. None the less, in individual patients the specific

Figure 2.1 The process of rehabilitation.

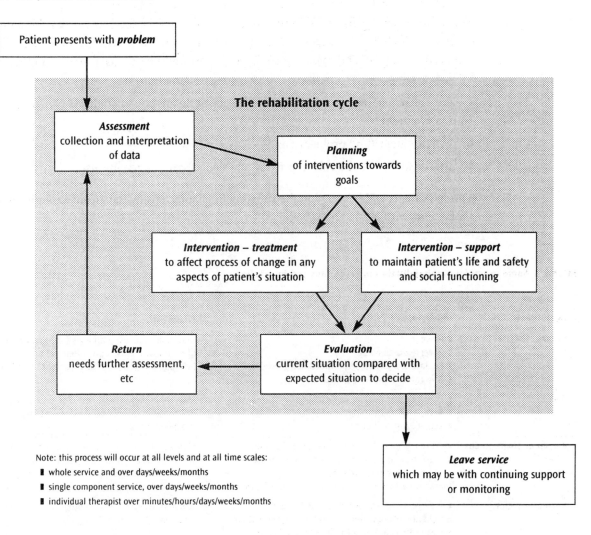

Patient presents with **problem**

The rehabilitation cycle

Assessment
collection and interpretation of data

Planning
of interventions towards goals

Intervention – treatment
to affect process of change in any aspects of patient's situation

Intervention – support
to maintain patient's life and safety and social functioning

Return
needs further assessment, etc

Evaluation
current situation compared with expected situation to decide

Leave service
which may be with continuing support or monitoring

Note: this process will occur at all levels and at all time scales:
▮ whole service and over days/weeks/months
▮ single component service, over days/weeks/months
▮ individual therapist over minutes/hours/days/weeks/months

combination of impairments may well be unique. Further, the disability that arises will vary even more, because the link between impairment and disability is also variable. Patients with spinal cord injury, who are often used as typical examples of patients with long-term disability, are in fact unusual because in complete injury the level of damage to the spinal cord quite closely determines the impairment and disability – but not the level of participation. Diagnoses themselves are therefore not useful in determining service need or resource allocation.

iii Given that disability may be generated or influenced by many different factors, the range of potential interventions is great. Indeed, it will be rare for only one or two interventions to be appropriate. In addition, a reasonable assessment is likely to require several experts, and there is evidence that single clinicians will miss important aspects of an individual's situation.[15] It is equally likely that the interventions needed will require input from several different professions. The effectiveness of stroke unit rehabilitation probably arises because a multiprofessional expert team is likely to identify most important factors impacting upon disability and to be able to resolve most of the resolvable problems.

Summary

2.14 This chapter has briefly overviewed a systematic framework for considering the nature and genesis of disability. It suggests that most patients with troublesome persistent disability will need assessment and management by an expert multidisciplinary team, and that isolated individual clinicians are not likely to be effective because they:

- are unlikely to have adequate knowledge about the disease to guide assessment and intervention;

- will not identify all problems; and

- will be unlikely to be able to provide all the necessary interventions.

2.15 This hypothesis will be tested in the subsequent chapters, using data from an audit of services for patients with MS in Oxfordshire.

Table 2.3 Some examples of rehabilitation interventions and interactions.

⊗ Level/term

Level of illness	Intervention	Comment
Organ	■ Prevent ■ Reverse or remove ■ Replace lost physiological function (eg insulin) ■ Give information and advice	Important to know pathology for prognosis and likely impairments. 'Cure' often not possible. (NB: pathology is not always present in an illness)
Person	■ Prevent occurrence or worsening of impairment ■ Reverse or improve impaired skill ■ Replace lost skill or part	May use therapy, drugs, orthoses, prostheses, etc. (NB: impairment may improve secondary to functional practice)
Person in environment	■ Prevent patient learning abnormal behaviours ■ Teach how to undertake activities in presence of immutable impairments ■ Practice activities, advising on risks, techniques, etc	Involves altering behaviour in one way or another. Will often also involve changing environment. May involve changing patient goals or goals of others. Takes time, and depends upon learning
Person in society	■ Prevent loss of social contacts and roles ■ Help identify new roles, and how to develop them ■ Ensure there are opportunities to develop or maintain roles	Will almost always involve other people. Takes a long time

⊗ Context of illness

Personal context	■ Prevent development of maladaptive beliefs and expectations ■ Alter beliefs and expectations if necessary, usually through giving information and psychological therapy	Beliefs and expectations are major determinants of behaviour, but consequences of behaviour may also affect beliefs and expectations
Physical context	■ Avoid loss of familiar environment if possible ■ Adjust environment physically, including through providing care	Could include orthoses, etc.
Social context	■ Adjust or help patient find new social context, or help adapt to new social context	Usually strongly linked to accommodation and work

⊗ Totality of illness

Quality of life	■ Full rehabilitation	Depends upon interventions at many levels

Note: almost all interventions depend upon active involvement and participation of patient and/or family.

Figure 2.2 Some of the influences on disability (alteration in activities). (Note: other arrows exist, and most are two-way)

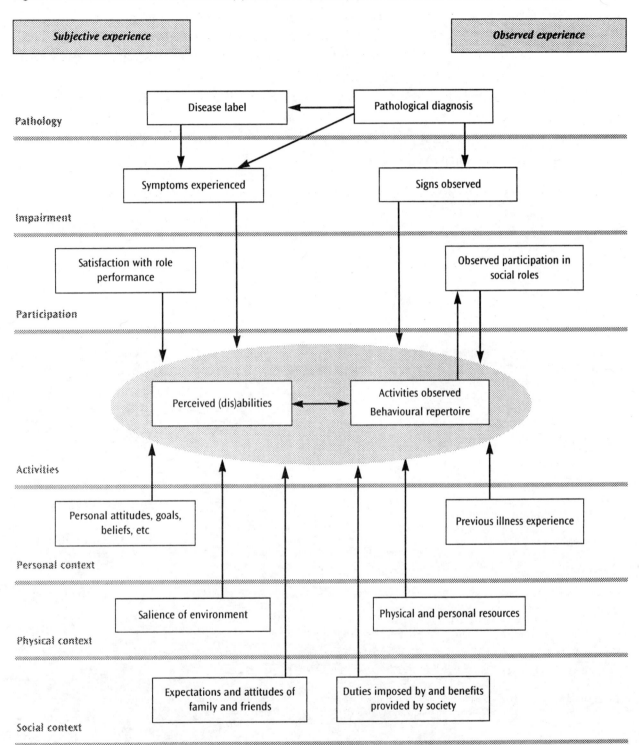

Part 2

The Oxfordshire Multiple Sclerosis Service Audit

3 Preliminary studies

3.1 This project broke new ground in that it aimed to investigate and audit all services delivered to a specific group of patients (those with multiple sclerosis (MS)), these services spanning many organisations, professions and geographical sites. Audit, in contrast to research, is a systematic attempt to improve specific local services, based as far as possible on evidence from research to set standards. Unfortunately, there was (and remains) minimal evidence that can be used to set appropriate standards for any of the services. Audit is also strongly related to specific local circumstances, so much preparation was needed before the audit could be commenced. This chapter summarises the results of our preparatory work.

3.2 Our initial intention had been to establish some agreed standards for the management of specific clinical problems, to measure service performance against those standards, and to feed back results with suggestions on how matters might be improved. To gain commitment to the audit, we undertook some preliminary work, expecting to identify six or more specific processes for audit.

Aim and objectives of the initial work

3.3 The *aim* of the initial work was to decide which existing services should be included and what standards might be applied, while the *objectives* were to consult widely with:

- all service providers (health and social services), to determine what they considered were reasonable standards for their service, and to establish their commitment to the audit;
- service users, to establish which services gave greatest cause for concern and what standards the users considered appropriate;
- service purchasers, to gain their views on appropriate standards and to establish their commitment to changing services if necessary; and
- individuals and organisations with specific or specialist knowledge or experience in the areas of MS services, to establish their concerns.

3.4 The first two steps were to determine:

i   What services were currently being offered within Oxfordshire for people with MS.

ii What issues and problems were considered most important regarding these services.

Preliminary study

3.5 In this preliminary phase, the researcher (QG) spoke to as many users, providers and purchasers as possible within Oxfordshire. There was also consultation with known experts in and outside Oxfordshire to learn about research into or audit of services going on elsewhere. The main method was direct interviews by the researcher but, in addition, an open meeting was held at Rivermead Rehabilitation Centre to discuss the problems. The results of this process were published in an initial report which was disseminated for local discussion at that time.

3.6 The main conclusions of this work were:

i Confirmation that services were not organised around the medical diagnosis of MS itself. No single service focused on patients with MS, and patients with MS were never the major group seen in any service.

ii It was obvious that no service could easily identify and monitor performance specifically in relation to patients with MS.

iii There was much general dissatisfaction with services, expressed not only by patients but also by service providers and service purchasers (though they chose not to be actively involved in the audit process).

3.7 The preliminary investigations also showed that:

▪ No measurable standards would be agreed because:

– purchasers did not participate actively in the consultation;

– providers of generic services were reluctant to set standards for a specific subgroup of patients; and

– patients and their families often had unrealistic expectations.

▪ In many areas, the standards suggested related primarily to the attitude of clinicians, not to measurable outcomes.

▪ One major weakness of services was the failure of a person or service even to recognise or acknowledge that the patient had a problem to be addressed, making it difficult to set a standard to which the service could aspire (confirming the hypothesis that a multidisciplinary team approach was needed for the initial assessment of a patient).

3.8 Therefore, it rapidly became clear that auditing particular services or events through routinely collected data would not be possible, and specific standards would not be agreed. Consequently, the initial design of the project had to be radically altered. We addressed a series of obstacles and, through this, an alternative approach to monitoring and improving quality (the goal of audit) was devised.

Problems identified and their solutions

3.9 Problems which had to be overcome in order to investigate the quality of services for patients with MS and how they might be improved included:

▪ the absence of any specific 'MS service' to be audited;

▪ establishing a register of people with MS willing to participate in the audit;

▪ estimating and confirming the number of patients;

▪ establishing the clinical context: developing a postal questionnaire to characterise the clinical status and problems experienced by patients;

▪ validating data collected;

▪ addressing problems arising in the process of making and telling the new diagnosis of MS (a specific area of concern identified by many patients);

▪ responding to practical problems identified during the audit (an ethical dilemma as the auditor was supposed to *observe* current services, not to *improve* them).

The absence of any specific 'multiple sclerosis service' to be audited

3.10 Oxfordshire is probably typical of most health authority areas in that patients with MS draw upon many services but rarely comprise a major part of any service's patient population. Our initial research established that services which were used to a reasonable degree by Oxfordshire patients with MS addressing problems related to MS included:

- Hospital medical services:
- neurology (outpatient, elective inpatient, emergency inpatient);
- general medicine (emergency inpatient);
- urology (outpatient).

- Day care services (social services, NHS).

- Respite care services (NHS specialist disability Young Disabled Unit, NHS community hospitals, voluntary sector Cheshire Homes, nursing homes, elsewhere).

- Disability-based services:
- wheelchair services (NHS, general and specialist);
- physiotherapy (hospital outpatient, community hospital, specialist disability centres, domiciliary, voluntary sector, etc);
- occupational therapy (NHS, social services);
- orthotics (NHS).

- Housing adaptations (housing, social services).

- Many others (eg the eye hospital).

3.11 These services spanned many different organisations, professions and locations within Oxfordshire:

- five NHS trusts;
- health (NHS) and social services;
- at least six different professional groups;
- over 30 different locations.

Method of audit

3.12 The traditional method of audit is to compare structure, process or outcome against standards.[16]

3.13 The *structure* of a service comprises its component parts and resources. In principle, the 'structure' could have been audited by first defining all the resources to which patients should have access, and then checking whether the resources were present. This was not done for several reasons:

- the totality of services that someone with MS might need is little different from the totality of services that the population might need;

- the presence of a service does not necessarily mean that someone with MS can access the service, but it is *access* that is of concern;

- no service specifically identified the use of that service by patients with MS.

Process and/or outcome

3.14 Auditing process and/or outcome depends upon data that relate to specific people who make contact with and use the service being audited. None of the services had a data system that could accurately and reliably identify patients with MS. It was clearly impractical to expect staff working within any service to collect data relating to their performance in managing patients with MS. In any case, data collection for audit will increase the workload on health professionals, recording when and where certain actions took place. It is also important to obtain the data reasonably promptly if change is to be implemented. Consequently, it was decided to use patients as 'probes', simply tracing their progress through the many systems and noting the problems revealed. Patients were asked to collect data using an audit card. The card was similar to that used in a study on diabetes care carried out within Ealing, Hammersmith and Hounslow Health Authority.[17] The card was used as a record of the performance of any service contacted, keeping a history of the process followed in resolving any problem. This technique gave a clear record of what clinical problems people were experiencing, who they were seeing for those problems, when they were being seen, and how they were treated. It therefore gave information on the services actually being used (structure) as well as how they were used (process) and the end result (outcome).

Establishing a register of people with multiple sclerosis willing to participate in the audit

3.15 It was vital to have a group of people prepared to have data collected about them because the health service data systems cannot reliably identify patients with MS. It was not legal to use the existing register of patients with MS at the Radcliffe Infirmary because those patients had not given permission for it to be used in this way (it was a research register within the department of neurology). A new register of willing volunteers was essential, and was recruited from several sources, including the local MS society through its meetings and newsletters, the general practitioners (GPs) who asked their patients, announcements in the media, word of mouth, etc. Each name on this new register was given by the patient him/herself. When signing permission for inclusion on the register they were also asked if they would like to receive information about other research projects through a newsletter. Most assented.

3.16 The register was clearly not epidemiologically complete but selected, only taking individuals who volunteered. The diagnosis was not checked formally by direct clinical assessment of every patient although, where possible, formal diagnosis was confirmed through records at the Radcliffe Infirmary (the local neurology centre) or held by the GP. All GPs were notified of the study and informed if any of their patients were added to the register. In all cases, it was understood that a diagnosis of MS had at some stage been given to the person concerned either directly or indirectly. Any patient known not to have MS was omitted from the study. In practice, the majority of patients were already known to the main medical investigator (DW). All addresses were checked to ensure that the individuals concerned lived within the Oxfordshire area. Probably over 95% of patients studied had clinically definite MS and few, if any, had an alternative diagnosis. It was not a major concern that a few patients may not have had MS because the intention was to audit services for individuals believed (by themselves and/or others) to have MS. The register was developed to include sufficient individuals so that over the course of the audit at least some of them would use most of the relevant services. Between February and December 1995, 230 people were registered. A computer database (Microsoft Access) was used to hold the register.

Estimating and confirming the number of patients

3.17 It was necessary to estimate the number of people with MS who lived in Oxfordshire. Estimates from published studies suggested an incidence of four new cases per 100,000 per year in the UK and a prevalence of 130 per 100,000 (ie all cases).[18,19] The population of Oxfordshire is about 590,000 (Office of Population Censuses and Surveys), so 24 new cases would be expected each year and 780 people living in Oxfordshire would be expected to have MS. To improve the validity of our study, the estimated total number of patients with MS calculated from published prevalence rates was compared with the number of people identified by a simple census of GPs.

3.18 During July and August 1995 all GPs who take Oxfordshire patients were asked to identify the number of people on their lists with a formal diagnosis of MS (usually given by a neurologist in Oxford). Of the 493 GPs approached (including those in the peripheral shires), 436 responded (12% non-response rate). The number of GPs per practice ranged from one to nine. There were 713 people with MS registered with responding GPs. The average (mean) numbers of patients with MS per GP and per GP practice were 1.63 and 6.48, respectively. It was assumed that the 57 GPs who did not respond also each had 1.63 people with MS, giving an additional 93 people with MS. Therefore, it was estimated that in 1995 approximately 800 (713 + 93) people living in Oxfordshire had a formal diagnosis of MS. This figure is close to the expected figure of 780 estimated from the most recent formal surveys.

3.19 This survey confirmed the number of patients that might use the services. Unfortunately, estimates of service need – or, indeed, of service use – are almost impossible to make from published data,[20] and no formal survey of need or service use had been carried out in Oxfordshire. Moreover, need (the ability to benefit from an intervention) is difficult to establish without assessing a patient.

Establishing the clinical context: developing a postal questionnaire to characterise the clinical status and problems experienced by patients

3.20 In contrast to most areas of clinical practice, patients with MS using services were not only likely to present with a great variety of clinical problems but also to have multiple and varied other relevant pre-existing impairments and disabilities and to come from a wide variety of contexts. To interpret any data arising from any contact with a service, it was felt necessary to have some background information on each individual, their medical state, social circumstances, disability level, etc. None of this could be obtained from notes: data in notes are inaccurate and incomplete, the work involved would have been considerable, and multiple permissions would have been required to undertake the work. In addition, it was necessary to know what problems were being experienced by people on the audit, to compare with problems recognised and resolved by the services being audited.

3.21 A postal questionnaire was developed to obtain this information directly from people with MS. Examination of existing scales and measures showed that they did not adequately cover all aspects of MS, so it was decided to design a disability status questionnaire for this study. (Since the study was finished the Guy's Neurological Disability Scale has been developed,[21] which might well be a useful alternative or addition.)

The Rivermead Disability Status Questionnaire

3.22 The Rivermead Disability Status Questionnaire (RDSQ) was designed as a self-administered assessment that could be mailed to people as required. It was intended to cover all the elements necessary to obtain a good picture of current problems and those that might be potential problems for the future. The content of the questionnaire was devised after a literature search of MS problems and potential problems, after consulting experts in the field of MS, and from conclusions drawn from the initial stages of the audit in Oxfordshire. The RDSQ was subjected to peer review by specialists in MS for face and content validity using a tested questionnaire.[22]

3.23 A pilot study of the questionnaire was carried out in 20 people with MS chosen randomly from the register to determine (to some extent) its reliability and utility. They were sent the questionnaire with a stamped addressed return envelope. After the questionnaire was returned, a visit by the researcher was arranged to complete the questionnaire using a face-to-face assessment and the same questions. A comparison of the answers on the postal questionnaire and at interview led to a number of changes in the questionnaire. The order of questions was changed, obvious mistakes corrected, and questions on important aspects of people's lives that had been omitted were added, including a whole section on sleep. It also became evident from the pilot study that the accuracy of the information could be increased if the questionnaire was filled out by the person with MS helped by a person who knew them well; this helped overcome errors due to memory problems, etc. The final draft of the RDSQ was then mailed to everyone on the register, except those who participated in the pilot. (A modified version for use with disabled patients referred from the community for rehabilitation is available from the authors.)

Validating data collected

3.24 Information given by people on the audit might have been unreliable or incomplete, for example dates can easily be forgotten or omitted. Several methods were used to clarify and confirm contacts and to validate symptoms/problems presented, the supply of equipment etc:

i   When notified about contact with a professional by a patient, the researcher contacted the professional concerned to seek confirmation of data. This was always attempted, although it was anticipated that in some cases it would be difficult to contact busy health professionals working in the community.

ii   Requests for equipment or adaptations during the audit were verified by confirming delivery dates or dates of installation through any health professionals concerned and/or the recipients of the equipment, etc.

3.25 Final confirmation of the number of people who did or did not experience new or worsening symptoms in their MS over the duration of the audit was achieved in two ways:

i   Since GPs are the primary source of referrals, a letter was sent in the tenth month to all the respondents' GPs asking them to supply a list of the occasions on which they saw or were contacted by the named patient and also the reason(s) patients were seen.

ii   A letter was sent to the people participating in the audit, asking whether they had made any contacts with anyone from the NHS or social services over the last 10 months (Yes or No), to confirm the non-contacts and allow for follow-up in the cases where contacts were missed.

Investigating the process of making the diagnosis

3.26   Initial investigation showed that dissatisfaction with the process of telling the diagnosis was very high. However, an audit eliciting information from volunteers using an audit card could be effective only in measuring those problems experienced by people who already had a diagnosis of MS, and could not include those currently going through the process of diagnosis. It is not practical to identify cases of suspected undiagnosed MS to follow their progress as it happens. A separate approach was needed, and a semi-structured interview was designed to elicit the required information.

Identifying newly diagnosed cases

3.27   There are a number of ethical and practical problems in approaching people who are recently or newly diagnosed. A small number of recently diagnosed patients were identified from the register, but an ongoing recruitment campaign was established throughout the audit to gain as many interviews as possible. The MS specialist nurse at the Radcliffe Infirmary NHS Trust in Oxford assisted by sensitively approaching individuals with whom she came in contact to join the project. Only people who had been diagnosed after January 1994 were approached (a maximum of two years after diagnosis) and consent obtained. An interview was requested, and in most cases the researcher visited the patients in their own homes. Of the 15 people approached, three contributed early in the project to the design of the semi-structured interview. They were unaware of how the interview schedule would be structured, and a considerable time (six months) elapsed prior to their formal interview.

Practical problems identified in the audit

3.28   In audit, the auditor is not normally expected to provide a service or in any way directly improve the service delivered. However, given the method being used in this audit, the researcher anticipated experiencing situations that might be ethically compromising, specifically if an urgent need was not being recognised or met. It was decided that if such situations arose the researcher would make a decision to intervene, but that interventions were to be as non-intrusive as possible. All interventions were recorded and have been listed in the results section.

Summary

3.29   The preliminary work showed that our initial idea of simply establishing some agreed standards and measuring services against those standards would not be practical. A method was developed which it was hoped would allow us to investigate the quality of services received by patients with MS.

4 | The audit: method

4.1 After the preliminary work described in Chapter 3 we had devised a methodology which was used for the main study carried out between 1st January 1996 and 1st November 1996. Active data collection ceased on the latter date, although data continued to filter in until December 1996. The audit was in two parts:

Part one – audit of services for people with an existing diagnosis of multiple sclerosis (MS).

Part two – interviews of those newly diagnosed with MS.

4.2 This chapter describes the methodology used and highlights some practical points. In essence, individual patients were used as probes and asked to report all contacts with any services for new problems. These contacts were then investigated. Newly diagnosed patients were interviewed about their experience of the process of diagnosis.

Identifying new service contacts

4.3 People from the register were mailed audit cards with a stamped addressed return envelope and a set of instructions detailing what needed to be done. The card encouraged them to note any *new* problem related to MS (or old problem that had worsened), and to record how it was handled (or otherwise) by services. It was decided not to ask patients about long-standing but static problems to prevent any confusion over problems that had already been or were currently being addressed at the beginning of the audit. Each person was responsible for filling in or having the audit card filled in whenever they had contact with someone from social services or the NHS.

4.4 A six-week pilot study of the audit card in 20 people showed that events tended to be reported only when the card had been totally completed, which led to a considerable delay between an event and its being reported. To reduce this delay, those participating in the main study were requested to telephone Rivermead Rehabilitation Centre (the central office for the audit) to notify the researcher each time they had contact with someone from the NHS or social services. This facilitated the whole process, and reporting to the audit was more regular and at a more suitable time. The card was still used as a written record of events. Each reported event was recorded by a secretary, and regular follow-up phone calls were made to check progress. The card was also modified after the pilot to allow more space for writing and the instructions on the card were made clearer.

4.5 The researcher attempted to phone every person at least twice during the audit period to prompt any who were slow in reporting events. This proved only partially successful because it was time-consuming and some people proved difficult to contact by phone during working hours. In some cases, phone calls had to be made in the evening. A core of people on the register consistently sent in their audit cards and kept contact, while others needed regular prompting.

4.6 None the less, the combination of cards, phone calls (patient-initiated, follow-up and routine monitoring) seemed to give a clear record of the clinical problems people were experiencing, who they were seeing for these problems, when they saw them, and how they were being treated. This method was used for the 10 months of the audit, testing the feasibility of the scheme and determining how long interest in reporting events could be maintained.

4.7 Initially, 150 people randomly chosen from the register were recruited to the audit. However, only 12 of them reported contacts between the start of the audit in January 1996 and the following March, so it was decided to add the remaining 85 people on the register to the audit. Any events that had occurred in the prior three months were quickly recorded and followed up to prevent confusion in the overall results.

Data validation and handling

4.8 The data collected during the audit were validated to ensure the accuracy of the information. Attempts to confirm any contacts with professionals were made by contacting the health professional concerned, but it was common to not get a response from letters and phone calls. Where equipment was involved, the act of delivery proved a good way of confirming equipment type, waiting times, etc. if contact could not be made with the health professional concerned. Sending letters to the patient and their general practitioner (GP) proved successful in confirming non-contacts and allowed for follow-up in the cases where contacts may have been missed.

4.9 These methods appear to have been successful. Preliminary analysis of the data collected several months into the audit confirmed that, while dates were not always accurate (sometimes out by a few days), reporting of events was usually fairly consistent. Follow-up was required only to confirm exact delivery dates of equipment, the outcomes of certain events such as visits to the GP, and the type of symptom(s) presented.

4.10 The data collected were difficult to categorise or classify, but the presenting problems were eventually grouped into one of 30 groups (see Chapter 5). Some problems were 'medical' but many were not. Furthermore, some patients presented with the same problem on more than one occasion (this was also noted). It was equally difficult to classify the service responses. There is currently no lexicon for accurately describing complex service interventions. Again, simple descriptive groups were used. In addition, extensive notes were kept about many individual patient problems, and used to give more qualitative detail.

Data categories

4.11 The categories used for the data collected and recorded included:
- the presenting (new) symptom or problem;
- the health professionals/services contacted;
- any problems with referrals (NHS or social services);
- specific problems with social services;
- equipment supply (including waiting times);
- benefits supplied;
- investigations required (including magnetic resonance imaging) and waiting times;
- any steroids required; and
- any problems with the audit technique.

4.12   The data were entered on a computer database (Microsoft Access) for analysis. The analytic method used was largely descriptive. The analysis took much longer than expected, mainly because of the amount and complexity of the data. There was no opportunity at this stage to feed data back in a structured way to complete the audit cycle. However, as recorded later, extensive changes in services were occurring anyway and these drew upon early informal results of the audit and audit process.

The semi-structured interview of the recently diagnosed

4.13   The content of the semi-structured interview was determined by impressions gained at the start of the project and by casual interviews carried out both with newly diagnosed people and with those diagnosed some years previously (see Chapter 6 for interview schedule). Three newly diagnosed people eligible for the main study were approached to ensure that appropriate and current questions were included. The answers from these three pilot interviews were included in the final analysis of patients who had been recently diagnosed.

4.14   The semi-structured interview schedule was subjected to review by a panel of six experts in the field of neurological rehabilitation to check face validity, and assessed for content and face validity using a tested questionnaire.[22] This necessitated minor changes in sentence construction and the order of the questions. The interviews were then tested on two people with a long-standing diagnosis of MS to ensure all points had been included. They were also asked to fill out the same questionnaire.

Summary

4.15   The method needed some modifications after the preliminary work. We needed to be proactive both in following up notified contacts and in checking whether any contact(s) had occurred. To give enough episodes of service contact, 226 patients were needed. The data collected were difficult to categorise, and pragmatic groups were used.

5 Results: main study

5.1 The method used, described in the last two chapters, gave a mass of unstructured information which was placed into groups. This seemed the most appropriate way of classifying the presenting problems or service actions. The results from the audit of the process of diagnosis are described in Chapter 6. This chapter gives:

i The results of the preliminary study. The Rivermead Disability Status Questionnaire (RDSQ) was used to establish the prevalence of symptoms and disabilities in our study population.

ii A descriptive analysis of most of the data collected during the audit.

Prevalence of symptoms and disability

5.2 The final draft of the RDSQ was mailed to everyone on the register (except those who participated in the pilot), 210 people in total, of whom 150 (71%) returned completed questionnaires:

- 27 (18%) were fully mobile, being able to run or walk fast for 10 metres without limping;
- 71 (47%) required some form of aid for mobility;
- 52 (35%) used a wheelchair all the time.

5.3 Symptoms shown in Table 5.1 caused problems all the time in the people who reported them (150 patients with multiple sclerosis (MS)). Mobility problems were the greatest single area of difficulty, closely followed by fatigue, sensory disturbance (including pain) and bladder disturbance. The frequency of swallowing problems (12%) is worth noting because this has only recently been recognised as a problem in MS. In contrast, the low frequency of self-reported cognitive deficits is notable given emerging evidence that cognitive deficits are common.

Prospective audit: population studied

5.4 Approximately one-quarter (235) of the total number of people with MS in Oxfordshire were approached for the audit; eight people did not wish to participate and one was found not to have a diagnosis of MS. The 226 people who agreed to participate (66 men (29%) and 160 women (71%)) were aged 25–85 years (mean (standard deviation (SD)) 50.2 (12.0) years). Duration of the disease ranged from 1–61 years (median 13.5 years; mean (SD) 17.1 (11.1) years). Seven people (3%) died during the 10 months of the audit and three moved away from Oxfordshire. Thirty-six people (16%) failed to respond during the study, although letters were sent to their general practitioners (GPs) to determine the number of times they had been seen. A total of 180 people (80%) maintained contact with the audit service and completed the audit.

▷ **All data presented hereafter comes from the 180 people who completed the 10-month audit (although data were also secured from GPs who volunteered information for the 36 people with whom contact was lost during the 10 months).**

Table 5.1 Prevalence of symptoms giving problems all the time in 150 patients with multiple sclerosis.

Problem area	Patients No.	%	Problem area	Patients No.	%
Control of legs	101	67	Eyes and eyesight	18	12
Control of balance	81	54	Swallowing	18	12
Fatigue	74	49	Remembering	15	10
Sensation (feeling)	49	33	Emotion (mood)		
Control of bladder	47	31	or control of emotion	13	9
Pain	42	28	Concentration	12	8
Control of arms	35	23	Speech	11	7
Muscle spasms	31	21	Thinking	10	7
Control of bowels	28	19			

5.5 Sixty-eight people (30%) had no contacts with anyone from the NHS or social services during the audit period, while 112 (50%) had some kind of contact through visits, letter or phone.

▷ **All percentages hereafter relate to the 226 people initially registered and agreeing to participate.**

Prospective audit: the presenting 'new' symptoms or problems

5.6 Contacts with services recorded during the audit were usually triggered by the occurrence of some worrying new physical or emotional symptom or problem that needed addressing. The data collected during the audit demonstrated that it is not always easy to distinguish MS related symptoms from those that are not, because physical symptoms of MS can mimic problems attributable to other disorders. For example, pain and loss of sensation in extremities may be due to MS but could easily be construed as an orthopaedic problem. The reverse is also true, in that symptoms from other diseases may mimic those of MS.

5.7 It was decided to record all reports of medical symptoms to gain a more comprehensive picture of what was presented. This may mean that some problems unrelated to MS have been included, for example where there was confusion as to the origin of such problems as 'hot flushes' or 'a chronic reduction in white blood cell count'. However, in most instances, MS was either a direct cause or had caused the situation to some extent (such as a fractured hip due to mobility problems caused by MS). In any event, both the patient and the GP or other professional might well incorrectly attribute the symptom to MS or, conversely, assume incorrectly that the problem was not due to MS. One or more presenting problems or symptoms were recorded by 117 patients over 10 months (Table 5.2). The 72 types of symptom or problem recorded have been grouped into 30 categories. In most cases, they were reported by the patient to a GP or other health professional, so many do not have obvious or precise labels or causes. Nevertheless, they reflect the problems actually experienced by patients, and represent those initially presented to health and other professionals.

5.8 The overall frequency of clinical (presenting) problems is shown in order of frequency in Table 5.2 (a breakdown of symptoms/problems, where appropriate, is given in Table 5.3), listing:

▓ the number of occurrences of the symptom or problem;

▓ the number of people presenting with that problem; and

▓ the number of people (within the total population) with more than one occurrence (two plus) or chronic symptoms (three or more occurrences reported) over the 10 months of the audit.

Table 5.2 Symptoms/problems presented during the 10-month audit period in 226 people with multiple sclerosis in order of frequency.

Symptom/problem	Total	No. of people	≥ 2 occ	Chronic
Urinary	78	39	18	6
Mobility	64	58	3	11
Advice required	49	25	8	
General deterioration	>40	30	9	
Gastrointestinal	36	26	3	1
Pain	32	24	5	
Respiratory	20	13	3	
Injury caused by trauma or fall	17	15	2	
Emotional	16	12	1	
Pressure areas	14	10	1	
Circulatory	9	9		
Swallowing/Speech	9	8	1	
Sensory (altered or loss in sensation)	7	6	1	
Fatigue (fatigue/lethargy/malaise)	7	6	1	
Gynaecological	7	6	1	
Loss of consciousness	7	3	1	
Musculo-skeletal	6	6		
Infection	4	4		
Activities of daily living (unable to wipe bottom)	1	1		
Medical certificate	3	2	1	
Vertigo	3	3		
Visual	3	3		
Social services referral required	3	3	1	
Hearing	2	1	1	
Cognitive	2	2		
Artificial feeding	1	1		
Paralysis (facial nerve palsy)	1	1		
Medical (low white blood cell count)	1	1		1
Nausea	1	1		
Drug-related	13	7		

Chronic = no. of patients with chronic problem (≥ 3 or more occurrences); 2+ occ = no. of patients reporting problem ≥ 2 times.

Urinary (Table 5.3)

5.9 Urinary problems were the most frequent single type of problem reported (78 occurrences). Urinary tract infections (UTIs) (>46) were separated from more general urinary problems (32) not confirmed as infection. Of the 39 people (17%) who reported urinary problems, seven had occurrences both of urinary problems (such as incontinence) and of UTIs. Eighteen people (8%) had more than one occurrence, of whom six (3%) reported chronic symptoms with three or more occurrences over the audit period.

5.10 A list of treatments needed as a result of urinary problems has also been included in Table 5.3 to demonstrate the various interventions used (other than antibiotic treatment for infection). These data highlight the frequency of bladder disturbance, emphasising the need for an effective continence and urology service.

Mobility (Table 5.3)

5.11 In total, 58 people (26%) reported 64 episodes of mobility problems, three of them reporting more than one occurrence, while one person's mobility problem can best be described as chronic. The problems took various forms:

- 23 people (10%) reported 27 instances of mobility problems associated with deterioration in walking ability, two of them reporting more than one episode;

- 19 episodes of muscle spasms were reported by 17 people (7.5%), with one person seeking help on more than one occasion;

- tremor/shaking of limbs (also described as jerky legs) was reported by six people (3%).

- six people (3%) reported six episodes of arm or leg weakness or inco-ordination;

- injury-free falls and foot drop were each reported by two people;

- contracture and corns on the feet were each reported by one person.

5.12 It is of note that these patients presented with a *change* in mobility, but that many also reported concurrent impairments which were probably the underlying cause. For example, the patients with muscle spasms probably had troublesome spasticity. Some of the patients presenting with specific symptoms (impairments) such as sensory disturbance may also have had an associated decrease in their mobility.

▷ **This further illustrates the need for a service which can assess fully, and identify, the underlying problem which may well need an intervention from another professional, or indeed from several professionals: for example, a doctor to prescribe antispasticity medication, a physiotherapist to give gait re-education, and an orthotist to provide an orthosis.**

Advice required (non-medical problems) (Table 5.3)

5.13 Patients also reported 'problems' of a non-medical nature. Advice or information on MS or its treatment was sought from a health professional by 25 people (11%) during the audit, eight of them more than once. Nine people (4%) sought advice or information specifically on MS on 16 occasions, while 16 people (7%) sought advice regarding medications, treatment or prescriptions to do with their MS.

General deterioration (Table 5.3)

5.14 Over 40 instances of 'general deterioration' were reported by 30 people (13%) of whom nine (4%) had more than one occurrence. This area clearly included many different and differing problems, but the category reflects the 'problem' presented to the service concerned. 'General deterioration' included four identified situations, again illustrating how patients present to services with diffuse problems that may need detailed expert assessment in order to provide the correct solution:

- 13 people (6%) reported symptoms associated with a relapse or progression of their MS on more than 20 occasions, seven (3%) reporting more than one occurrence.

- 15 people (7%) reported general deterioration, 10 (4%) of them requiring more home care (two more than once) and five (2%) requiring respite.

- two people reported relapse or progression in their level of disability and general deterioration that required more home care.

Gastrointestinal (Table 5.3)

5.15 There were 36 instances of gastrointestinal problems reported by 26 people (12%). Three people had more than one occurrence, and in one the problems were chronic. Abdominal distension was reported four times by the same person, while 22 problems with defecation/bowel problems were recorded by 16 people (7%), in one of whom the problems were report-

Table 5.3. Breakdown of symptoms/problems presented during the 10-month audit period in 226 people with multiple sclerosis in order of frequency.

Symptom/problem	Total	No. of people	≥ 2 occ	Chronic
Urinary:	**78**	**39**	**18**	**6**
general (eg frequency)	32	25	5	1
UTI (haematuria)	>46	21	13	5
both problems reported	0	7	0	0
treatment needed:	15	12	2	
starts self catheterisation ISC	3	3	0	
starts urethral catheter while on audit	2	2	0	
problems with urethral catheter (eg blocked)	8	6	2	
suprapubic catheter inserted	2	2	0	
Mobility:	**64**	**58**	**3**	**1**
walking ability deteriorating	27	23	2	
muscle spasms	19	17	1	
arm or leg weakness/inco-ordination	6	6		
tremor/shaking of limb(s)/jerky legs	6	6		
falls with no associated injury	2	2		
foot drop	2	2		
contractures developing	1	1		
corns on feet	1	1		
Advice required (non-medical):	**49**	**25**	**8**	
advice or information about MS	16	9	3	
advice regarding medications/treatment or prescription	33	16	5	
General deterioration:	**>40**	**30**	**9**	
symptoms associated with a relapse or progression	>20	13	7	
general deterioration requiring more home care	13	10	2	
both the above	2	2	0	
general deterioration requiring respite	5	5	0	
Gastrointestinal:	**36**	**26**	**3**	**1**
general	10	9	1	
abdominal distension	4	1	1	
defecation/bowel	22	16	1	1
Pain:	**34**	**23**	**5**	
muscular pain	14	8	1	
neurogenic pain (eg burning)	15	11	4	
trigeminal neuralgia	3	3	0	
otalgia	1	1	0	
headaches	1	1	0	
Respiratory:	**20**	**13**	**3**	
general	1	1	0	
pneumonia	1	1	0	
chest infection	16	10	3	
catarrh	2	1		
Emotional:	**16**	**12**	**1**	
low in mood	5	5	0	
depression	10	6	1	
panic attacks/anxiety	1	1	0	
Circulatory:	**9**	**9**	**0**	
oedema (legs)	3	3	0	
raised blood pressure	1	1	0	
cold feet	2	2	0	
cramps	3	3	0	

Table 5.3 continued

Table 5.3. *continued*

Symptom/problem	Total	No. of people	≥ 2 occ	Chronic
Swallowing/speech:	9	8	1	
swallowing	6	5	0	
speech	1	1	0	
loss of taste/smell	1	1	0	
not eating	1	1	0	
Gynaecological:	7	6	1	
vaginitis	2	2	0	
hot flushes (gynaecological)	1	1	0	
sweats/shakes	2	2	0	
Candida albicans	2	1	0	
Social services referral required:	3	3	1	
financial worries	1	1	0	
main carer unable to cope necessitating home assistance	2	2	0	

Chronic = no. of patients with chronic problem (≥3 or more occurrences); 2+ occ = no. of patients reporting problem ≥2 times; ISC = intermittent self-catheterisation; UTI = urinary tract infection.

ed as chronic. Some of these problems may not have been related to the MS, but constipation and faecal incontinence are likely to have been. This illustrates the difficulty in separating out services and problems, given that although gastrointestinal symptoms are not obviously neurological impairments they often arise from the neurological disease.

Pain (Table 5.3)

5.16   Twenty-three people (10%) reported pain on 32 occasions, five (2%) reporting pain more than once. The types of pain experienced were:

- neurogenic pain, such as burning in one or more areas of the body: 11 people (5%) reported 15 episodes, four more than once;

- muscular pain: eight people (3.5%) reported 14 instances, one person more than once;

- trigeminal neuralgia: three people on three occasions (one of these people also experienced neurological pain in the legs on two occasions separate from the trigeminal neuralgia);

- otalgia and headaches were each reported by one person.

Respiratory (Table 5.3)

5.17   Twenty instances of respiratory problems were reported by 13 people (6%), of whom three reported more than one episode:

- chest infection: 16 instances in 10 people (4%);

- one person reported two episodes of difficulty with catarrh;

- one person had pneumonia;

- one instance of 'a general respiratory problem' (reported in this way by the GP).

Injury caused by trauma or fall

5.18   Fifteen people (7%) reported injury due to trauma or falls on 17 occasions, usually arising after episodes of overbalancing on to furniture or falling out of bed.

Emotional (Table 5.3)

5.19 Emotional problems were reported by 12 people (5%), one of whom experienced five occurrences of depression, giving 16 episodes in total. Emotional problems divided into three types:

■ five people (2%) reported five occurrences of feeling low in mood;

■ depression (as classified by the GP): six people (3%) reported 10 occurrences;

■ panic attacks/anxiety: one person sought help on one occasion.

Pressure areas

5.20 Fourteen instances of problems with pressure sores were reported by 10 people (4%). One person suffered four pressure areas due to ill-fitting leg splints. Three people contracted their pressure sores while in hospital.

Circulatory (Table 5.3)

5.21 Nine people (4%) reported nine instances described as 'problems with blood circulation', three reported leg oedema, one person was diagnosed as having raised blood pressure, two experienced cold feet, and three people reported episodes of muscle cramps.

Swallowing/speech (Table 5.3)

5.22 Eight people (3.5%) reported nine problems with swallowing or speech, one of whom had a recurrence of the problem. The problems included:

■ swallowing difficulties in six people (one person had a recurrence);

■ one person reported a speech problem;

■ one person reported loss in taste and smell (probably more a sensory problem);

■ there was one instance of not eating related to a swallowing problem, though not necessarily serious enough to impair eating.

Sensory (Table 5.3)

5.23 Problems with sensation included all reported episodes of altered sensation or sensory loss (pain has been considered separately). Seven instances of sensory disturbance were reported by six people (3%). In all these cases the patient clearly presented with sensory symptoms (an impairment) rather than a disability. It is possible that they had a concurrent worsening in disability which they did not put down as the presenting problem.

Fatigue

5.24 Fatigue was described in different ways, including lethargy and malaise. Seven instances of newly troublesome fatigue were reported by six people (3%).

Gynaecological (Table 5.3)

5.25 Though not specifically MS related, four types of gynaecological problems were reported. Six people (3%) reported seven instances of gynaecological problems, of which one person had more than one occurrence. The subcategories included:

■ two cases of vaginitis reported by two people;

■ one case of hot flushes;

- sweats/shakes: two people reported two cases;
- two episodes of *Candida albicans* in one person.

Loss of consciousness

5.26   Loss of consciousness was reported by three people (1%) who experienced seven episodes. One instance was of unknown origin. Six were due to a seizure; they were reported by two people, one of whom had more than three seizures.

Musculo-skeletal

5.27   Six people (3%) reported six instances of musculo-skeletal problems such as a frozen shoulder or a torn muscle.

Infection

5.28   Four infections (excluding UTIs and chest infections) were reported by four people (2%). There was one case each of balanitis and conjunctivitis, and two of viral illness.

Activities of daily living

5.29   One person was unable to wipe their bottom, and advice was sought through the GP.

Medical certificate

5.30   Two people had requested a medical certificate on three occasions.

Vertigo

5.31   Three people reported episodes of vertigo (2) or dizzy spells (1) on three occasions. The functional (disabling) consequences of this impairment, if any, are not recorded.

Visual

5.32   Three people reported visual problems on three occasions. One case was specifically optic neuritis, while the remaining two cases were non-specific, such as blurred vision.

Social services referral required (Table 5.3)

5.33   Three people reported wanting help from social services. Two of them asked for home assistance when a main carer became ill or was unable to cope, and one asked for assistance because of financial worries.

Hearing

5.34   One person reported problems with hearing on two occasions. It was diagnosed as a problem related to MS, though this is very rare.

Cognitive

5.35   Two people reported cognitive problems: one experienced memory problems, and the other confusion and forgetfulness. This low rate of reporting cognitive problems contrasts with the known high prevalence of cognitive problems in people with MS.

Feeding

5.36 One person experienced problems on one occasion with artificial feeds requiring assessment from a dietitian.

Facial paralysis

5.37 One person reported facial nerve palsy. This may have been an incidental Bell's palsy or possibly a relapse of MS. Further investigation was not undertaken.

Medical

5.38 There was an isolated case of raised white blood cell count of undetermined origin (despite testing) which persisted for the duration of the audit.

Nausea

5.39 Nausea was reported by one person.

Drug-related symptoms

5.40 Some people experienced symptoms from the drug treatment given for presenting problems. Thirteen instances of drug-induced side effects or symptoms were reported by seven people (3%), in all cases necessitating stopping or changing medications. The side effects or symptoms experienced included problems with defecation, general deterioration and mobility (specifically walking), muscle spasms, visual problems and *C. albicans*.

Comparison of incidence and prevalent problems

5.41 Many patients had problems at the outset. Their frequency in a sample of 150 was shown in Table 5.1. The frequency of new problems in these areas is compared with the prevalence of symptoms giving problems all the time in Table 5.4. Consultation rates were generally lower

Table 5.4. Prevalence of symptoms/problems before, and incidence during, the audit.

Problem area	Before audit		During audit	
	n = 150	%	n = 226	%
Control of legs	101	67	>58*	>25
Control of balance	81	54	*	
Fatigue	74	49	6	3
Sensation (feeling)	49	33	6	3
Control of bladder	47	31	25	11
Pain	42	28	23	10
Control of arms	35	23	>6*	
Muscle spasms	31	21	17	7
Bowel control	28	19	17	7
Eyes and eyesight	18	12	3	1
Swallowing	18	12	5	2
Remembering	15	10	1	<1
Emotion (mood) or control of emotion	13	12	9	5
Concentration	12	8	0	
Speech	11	7	1	<1
Thinking	10	7	1	<1

* difficult to determine.

than the prevalence rates (as would be expected), with consultations about sensory disturbance and fatigue particularly low.

People and services used

5.42 A record of all contacts with health professionals or specialist services was kept during the audit. Table 5.5 lists these in order of frequency (including the number of contacts made with the audit researcher). The results demonstrate both the large number of different people contacted by people with MS and the number of contacts required to seek a solution to any problems presented. The commonest contact was with GPs, both in terms of number of people making contact and in terms of number of contacts. Contacts with the audit researcher (through necessary intervention) were fourth highest in this list (see interventions by the researcher). The contacts and the reasons for them are discussed in detail below in order of frequency.

Table 5.5. Health service and other professionals contacted by 226 people with MS during the 10-month audit period.

Health professional or service	No. of people	No. of contacts
Doctors		
General practitioners	104	413
Consultants or specialist doctors*	69	90
Other professionals		
Social services occupational therapist	28	58
Audit researcher	25	32
District or practice nurse	22	47
Hospital-based physiotherapist	20	26
Hospital admission	19	28
Research physiotherapist (for gait therapy)	9	>50
Social services social worker	9	10
Community physiotherapist	8	9
MS specialist nurse	7	14
Mary Marlborough Centre (specialist disability service)	7	11
Oxfordshire Wheelchair Service	7	8
Care manager	6	12
Speech and language therapist	6	10
Ritchie Russell House (young disabled unit)	6	10
Hospital-based occupational therapist	6	9
Orthotics	5	14
Continence advisory service	5	7
X-ray department	3	4
Podiatry	3	3
Social services benefits office	3	3
Dietitian	2	3
Hospital-based social worker	2	3
Pain clinic	2	1
Clinical psychologist	1	>3
Accident and emergency department	1	2
Department of Social Security	1	2
Admission to nursing home	1	1
NHS dentist	1	1
Berkshire Wheelchair Service	1	1
Aylesbury Wheelchair Service	1	1

* for details of consultants contacted see Table 5.6

Contacts with doctors

General practitioners

5.43   Over the audit period there were 413 known contacts with GPs involving 104 people (46%):

   ▧   36 people (16%) either phoned or were phoned by their GP;

   ▧   41 (18%) made contact only for a check-up;

   ▧   there were 47 home visits by the GPs.

5.44   Four GPs admitted that they did not always record the visits they made. In three cases it was difficult to determine exactly how many visits were made because the person was seen regularly to solve a specific problem. Information on eight contacts was not complete either because not all the information was received before the end of the audit or it was unavailable to the researcher.

Hospital consultants (Table 5.6)

5.45   The commonest contact with a hospital specialist was with a consultant in neurological disability (also a neurologist): 27 people (12%) made contact on 31 occasions. One of these was only for a check-up and one contact was by letter (included in list below). Contacts with a neurologist were the next most common, and contacts with other specialists (including a consultant in rehabilitation) were infrequent. There were 27 known visits to a neurologist at the Radcliffe Infirmary (two of which the researcher was unable to verify) involving 16 people (7%). Four neurologists were contacted by telephone for advice by the GP. Eight people (3.5%) saw their neurologist only for a check-up. In one instance, information about the visit was not complete because not all the information was received before the end of the audit (included in the list below).

5.46   Patients visited or contacted many other consultants or specialist doctors, but each consultant or specialty only saw a few patients with MS, dramatically illustrating the huge range of services involved with patients with the condition.

Table 5.6. Contacts with consultants or specialist doctors by 226 people with MS during the 10-month audit period.

Consultant/hospital specialty	No. of people	No. of contacts
Consultant in neurological disability	27	31
Neurologist at the Radcliffe Infirmary	16	27
Surgical consultant	5	6
Urology consultant	6	6
Medical consultant	4	4
Specialist in sexual problems	1	4
Geratologist	1	3
Rehabilitation consultant	2	2
Neurosurgeon	1	1
Psychiatric consultant	1	1
Ear, nose & throat consultant	1	1
Consultant ophthalmologist	1	1
Orthopaedic consultant	1	1
Gastroenterologist	1	1
Maxillofacial surgery & orthodontics department	1	1

Contacts with other professionals (Table 5.5)

5.47 Patients were also in contact with many other people about their problems, again illustrating the huge range of people and services involved. The contacts have been listed in order of frequency of known or reported contacts.

Social services occupational therapist

There were 58 contacts with a social services occupational therapist (OT) (not in the capacity of a care manager) by 28 people (12%). Five people (2%) were in regular contact to solve a particular problem, two people made phone calls for advice, and two calls were check-ups by the OT to see if there were any problems.

Audit researcher

Of necessity, there were many contacts with the audit researcher.

District or practice nurse

There were 47 contacts with a district or practice nurse by 22 people (10%). Eight of these people were seen regularly (usually by a district nurse) for a period of time to solve a particular problem.

Hospital-based physiotherapist

There were 26 contacts with a hospital based physiotherapist by 20 people (9%). One of them was a home visit, and 12 saw the physiotherapist regularly to solve a particular problem.

Hospital admission

There were 28 hospital admissions over the audit period by 19 people (8%), with a duration of stay from one night to $3^{1/2}$ months.

Research physiotherapist (for gait therapy)

Nine people (4%) became involved in a research project which started during the audit in January 1996 and, as a consequence, received regular physiotherapy when normally they would not have received it. Four of them also received community or hospital physiotherapy during the audit period.

Social services social worker

There were 10 contacts with a social services social worker (not in the capacity of a care manager) by nine people (4%). Two people saw the social worker regularly for a short period of time to solve a particular problem, and four contacts were only to check for any problems.

Community physiotherapist

There were nine contacts with a community based physiotherapist by eight people (3.5%). Two people saw a physiotherapist regularly for a short period of time to solve a particular problem.

Multiple sclerosis specialist nurse

There were 14 contacts with the MS specialist nurse at the Radcliffe Infirmary by seven people (3%), six of them as part, or as a result, of a drug trial on which the MS specialist nurse was also working.

Mary Marlborough Centre (specialist disability service)

There were 11 visits to the Mary Marlborough Centre by seven people (3%). The researcher was unable to verify one visit, and one person saw the professional concerned regularly over a short period of time to solve a particular problem. The Mary Marlborough Centre offers specialist assessment and advice on aids and equipment including specialist wheelchairs.

Oxfordshire Wheelchair Service

There were eight contacts with the Oxfordshire Wheelchair Service by seven people (3%). One contact was by phone only to ask for advice.

Care manager

There were 12 contacts with a care manager (social services) by six people (3%). A care manager may be a social services OT, but these visits were recorded in the capacity of a care manager when people needed a review or assessment of care.

Speech and language therapist

There were 10 contacts with an NHS speech and language therapist by six people (3%).

Ritchie Russell House (specialist neurological disability service)

There were 10 contacts with new problems recorded by six people (3%) relating to Ritchie Russell House (RRH), the Oxfordshire 'Young Disabled Unit'. Many people attend RRH for regular review or treatment, as well as for day care and respite care, so it is likely that many problems identified and resolved by staff through regular review will not have been detected by this audit.

Hospital-based occupational therapist

There were nine contacts with a hospital based OT by six people (3%), one of whom saw the professional regularly to solve a particular problem over a short period of time, and three contacts were home visits.

Orthotics

There were 14 contacts with the orthotics service by five people (2%). One person saw the professional concerned regularly over a short period of time to solve a particular problem.

Continence advisory service

There were seven contacts with the continence advisory service (CAS) in Witney by five people (2%), one of whom was seen regularly over a period of time to solve a particular problem. It should be noted that 13 people were also visited by a district nurse in the capacity of a continence advisor with links to the CAS.

X-ray department

There were four contacts with an X-ray department (all at the John Radcliffe Hospital) by three people.

Podiatry

There were three visits to an NHS podiatrist by three people.

Social services benefits office

There were three contacts with the social services benefits office by three people.

Dietitian

There were three contacts with a dietitian by two people, one of them regularly over a period of time to solve a particular problem.

Hospital based social worker

There were three contacts with a hospital based social worker by two people. One person saw the social worker regularly over a period of time to solve a particular problem.

Pain clinic

There were two contacts with the pain clinic by one person.

Clinical psychologist

There were many contacts with a clinical psychologist by one person. The exact number of visits was not readily available, but this person was seen regularly over a period of time to solve a particular problem.

Accident and emergency department

One person made two visits to the accident and emergency department at the John Radcliffe Hospital in Oxford.

Department of Social Security

There were two contacts with the Department of Social Security (DSS) by one person.

Admission to nursing home

One person was admitted permanently to a nursing home during the period of the audit.

NHS dentist

There was one (home) visit by an NHS dentist. Those who saw an NHS dentist may not have thought to have recorded this as part of the audit. (Most people tended to have a private dentist.)

Wheelchair services

There was one contact each with the Berkshire and Aylesbury wheelchair services.

Equipment supply and repair (Table 5.7)

5.48 There were 61 requests for equipment during the audit period by health professionals. In one case a self-referral was made, but the department concerned took action as a result of that self-referral. Not all the requests were necessarily made on separate occasions. Multiple pieces of equipment were often ordered at one time, but for ease of description requests have been separated to allow for categorisation. The waiting times shown in Table 5.7 are the times after requests were made for equipment by the health professionals concerned; they do not include the time for the professional to make an assessment at the request of individuals with MS: for example, if an OT was contacted by someone with a problem, the time required for the OT to assess the appropriateness of this request was not always easily determined or verified. In some cases, a visit was initiated by the health professional (such as a social services OT) if needs were identified during routine check-up. Therefore, visits were not necessarily initiated by the person concerned recognising a problem or need.

The equipment requested was to meet the needs of 36 people (16%) participating in the audit. Twelve people (5%) required more than one piece of equipment (which was ordered during the audit period), two of them requiring up to five.

Eight types of equipment were identified and placed into categories for description. The eighth category relates to equipment orders arising out of an MS physiotherapy trial being carried out at the same time. The categories identified were:

▓ wheelchair or wheelchair/seating equipment;

▓ bathroom or toilet equipment;

▓ walking aids or splints;

▓ hoists or associated hoist equipment;

▓ hand rails or banisters;

▓ kitchen equipment;

▓ T-rolls (a piece of equipment); and

▓ aids supplied on the MS physiotherapy trial.

Table 5.7. Reported equipment supplied or needing repair during the 10-month audit period.

Type of equipment requested	No. of requests
Wheelchair or wheelchair/seating equipment	17
Bathroom or toilet equipment	12
Walking aids or splints	8
Hoists or associated hoist equipment	7
Hand rails or banisters	5
Kitchen equipment	3
T-rolls*	3
Aids supplied on physiotherapy research study	6

*A piece of equipment.

The main focus for equipment supply and repair was the waiting times required (Tables 5.8–5.14). Reasons for long waiting times were sometimes volunteered, as was other information about supply of equipment. These have been listed at the end of each table, which also shows the equipment supplied or needing repair during the audit period.

Hoists or associated hoist equipment (Table 5.8)

Five requests were made for ceiling hoists (six hoists), with a waiting time from 14 days to 6½ months. A specialist sling for a hoist required 5½ months for delivery due to the complex nature of the problem, and the commercial supply company took over three months to respond to a request for a hoist control to be repaired.

Hand rails or banisters (Table 5.9)

There were five requests for hand rails or a banister, with a range of waiting times from the next day to over three months.

Bathroom or toilet equipment (Table 5.10)

There were three requests for a shower chair, with waiting times of 12 days or less. In another case, a shower chair footplate requested from the commercial supply company took over three months to be supplied. Two commodes were ordered; one was delivered the same day, but the waiting time for the second was not determined. The remaining items in this category were one-off items that were supplied within two weeks or less of being ordered.

Kitchen equipment (Table 5.11)

Four items of equipment were ordered, with waiting times from seven days to seven months (for a mobile tray).

Wheelchair or wheelchair/seating equipment (Table 5.12)

Nine (non-electric) wheelchairs of varying types were ordered during the audit, with waiting times ranging from one week to over one year. Five other assorted wheelchair equipment items were ordered (including one Jay seating system ordered with one of the new wheelchairs); the waiting times for these ranged from the same day to three months. Two raised armchairs (one requested for seating) were requested and took 12 days to deliver.

Walking aids or splints (Table 5.13)

Three ankle/foot orthoses (AFOs) were ordered, supply of which ranged from the same day to four months. Three specialist items were ordered in the form of a leg caliper, refit of full leg splints and special shoes. Supply of these took between seven weeks and seven months. Two walking aids were supplied within 12 days or less.

T-rolls (Table 5.14)

Three T-rolls were requested; supply ranged from the same day to over six months.

Tables 5.8–5.14.
Waiting times for the supply and repair of equipment requested by 226 patients with MS over the 10-month audit period.

Table 5.8. Hoists or associated hoist equipment

Type of equipment	Department	Waiting time
1. Ceiling hoist	OTSS	4 months
2. Ceiling hoist	OTSS	?
3. Ceiling hoist	OTSS	14 days
4. Ceiling hoist	OTSS	6^1/2 months
5. Two ceiling hoists needed	OTSS	8 weeks
6. Specialised sling for hoist	OTSS, CS	5^1/2 months
7. Electric hoist control needed attention	OTSS, CS	>3 months

Comments offered on supply of hoists or associated hoist equipment:

3. Second-hand hoist used.
4. Hoist first requested 8.95. Formal assessment 12.2.96. Trial model fitted 19.4.96 to assess the type needed, disassembled and taken away on the same day. Ordered hoist arrived 28.8.96.
5. Loan hoist from hospital used immediately, so a hoist was available until requested hoists were installed.
6. It took 5^1/2 months to solve the sling problem. The OT worked hard to convince the commercial supplier that the problem could be solved, but the latter failed to keep contact over many weeks and had to be chased by the OT.

CS = commercial supplier of equipment; OT = occupational therapist; OTSS = occupational therapist employed by social services.

Table 5.9. Hand rails or banisters

Type of equipment	Department	Waiting time
Banister to stairs and hand rails	OTSS	4 days
Rails needed in passage way	OTSS	next day
Two grab rails	OTSS, PT(Com)	12 days
Hand rail and door intercom	OTSS	4 days
Extra handrail in washroom*	PT(Com)	>3 months

* had not been installed by the end of the audit 1.11.96.

OT = occupational therapist; OTSS = occupational therapist employed by social services; PT = physiotherapist; PT(Com) = physiotherapist working in the community.

Table 5.10. Bathroom or toilet equipment

Type of equipment	Department	Waiting time
New shower chair	OTSS	12 days
Shower chair	OTSS	2 days
Shower chair	OTSS	7 days
Shower chair footplate	OTSS, CS	>12 weeks
Shower commode*	OTSS	?
Commode	OTSS	same day
Bath seat	OTSS	3 days
Bath stool	OTSS	>2 weeks
New bathboard required	OTSS	2 weeks
Leaking shower needed repair	OTSS	next day
Raised seat for toilet	OTSS	2 weeks
Extender arm device to assist wiping bottom**	OTSS	Next day

Comments offered on supply of bathroom or toilet equipment:
* seat size changed twice after being supplied, but the person does not use the seat as it is too painful for their spine.
** the device was unsuccessful, and no other options were offered.

CS = a commercial supplier of equipment; OTSS = occupational therapist employed by social services.

Table 5.11. Kitchen equipment

Type of equipment	Department	Waiting time
Kitchen chair	OTSS	12 days
Kettle pourer & sticky mat for tray	OT(NHS)	7 days
Mobile tray required*	OTSS	7 months

* the tray was a one-off speciality item and therefore took longer to be supplied.

OT(NHS) = occupational therapist in NHS employment; OTSS = occupational therapist employed by social services.

Table 5.12. Wheelchair or seating equipment

Type of equipment	Department	Waiting time
1. New W/C	RRH PT, OTSS	1 month
2. New W/C	OWS, MMC	5½ months
3. Fold-up W/C	OTSS	<2 weeks
4. Self-propelling W/C	BWS	same day
5. W/C	AWS	>1 year
6. New W/C & Jay system	OWS	19 days
7. New self-propelled W/C required	OTSS	1 week
8. Lightweight W/C needed for independence	OTSS, OWS	12 days
9. Chair ordered after W/C assessment	OWS	6½ weeks
10 New cushion and back for W/C	OTSS	same day
11. Adjustment to W/C headrest needed	OWS	17 days
12. Pressure-relieving cushion	OTSS, OWS	same day
13. New sides to W/C	OTSS, OWS	3 months
14. Various adaptations to W/C after assessment	OWS	5 weeks
15. Special W/C cushion & back	RRH PT	same day
16. W/C cushion	self-referral OWS	4 days
17. 2 raised armchairs	OTSS, PT	12 days

Comments offered on supply of wheelchair or wheelchair/seating equipment:

5 The problems (mainly due to the W/C company) commenced in summer 1995, but have been recorded because of the unusual nature of supply problems: faulty chair supplied initially, and failure (twice) to make an appointment with the person concerned for supply of chair.

6 It took three months for an assessment after referral, and then 19 days to supply the chair.

8 The original request was made to the OTSS in August 1995, but the OWS said none were available due to a lack in funding. The community PT then phoned OWS to persuade them to give an appointment. The person was seen on 20.4.96.

9 The W/C arrived at the OWS but, because of a mix up, it was delivered to the person's home without an appointment (1.10.96). It was finally delivered on 8.10.96. The headrest was still not right by the end of the audit.

12 After taking a long time to be supplied, the chair was too big for the person's bungalow. An appropriate chair arrived the next day.

13 The technician did a home visit at 2½ months, but the sides of the chair he brought were wrong for the W/C.

14 From actual request through OTSS to supply was five months.

16 Someone at the OWS tried to put the person off, stating that the type of cushion requested was scarce. The person persisted and mentioned their participation in the OMSSA. The cushion was supplied.

AWS = Aylesbury Wheelchair Service; BWS = Berkshire Wheelchair Service; MMC = Mary Marlborough Centre (specialist disability service); OMSSA = Oxfordshire Multiple Sclerosis Service Audit; OTSS = occupational therapist employed by social services; OWS = Oxfordshire Wheelchair Service; PT = physiotherapist.; RRH = Ritchie Russell House (young disabled unit); W/C = wheelchair.

Table 5.13. Walking aids or splints

Type of equipment	Department	Waiting time
1. AFO	PT(Com),DN	4 months
2. AFO	PT, Orthotics	1 month
3. AFO	PT, Orthotics	same day
4. Leg caliper required	PT, Orthotics	3 1/2 months
5. Refit full leg splints	PT, Orthotics	7 months
6. Special shoes needed	Orthotics, RRH PT	>7 weeks
7. Indoor walking aid	PT(Com)	2 days
8. Walking frame	OTSS, PT(Com)	12 days

Comments offered on supply of walking aids or splints:

1   AFO splint did not fit.

4   The person was assessed and measured, but had to phone up 3 1/2 months later to find out what was happening - to be told that the caliper had been lost during a move to a new building. The file was found later that day, and a follow-up appointment was made one week later when the person received the caliper.

5   Leg splints needed remoulding. This was a particularly difficult problem because the person concerned was experiencing night spasms as well as having increased leg size due to a recent input of physiotherapy (extra muscle bulk) which caused pressure areas to develop on the legs.

6   The original referral went missing. The only excuse offered was that 'this happens from time to time'.

AFO = ankle foot orthosis (foot drop splint); DN = district nurse; OTSS = occupational therapist employed by social services; PT = physiotherapist; PT(Com) = physiotherapist working in the community; RRH PT = physiotherapist at Ritchie Russell House (young disabled unit).

Table 5.14. T-rolls

Type of equipment	Department	Waiting time
1. T-roll previously supplied was not right*	OTSS, MMC	>6 months
2. T-roll	PT(Com), DN	15 days
3. T-roll	RRH PT	same day

* request for review 6.2.96; finally reviewed six months and one week later.

DN = district nurse; MMC = Mary Marlborough Centre (specialist disability service); OTSS = occupational therapist employed by social services; PT(Com) = physiotherapist working in the community; RRH PT = physiotherapist at Ritchie Russell House (young disabled unit).

Mobility aids supplied during the research physiotherapy trial (Table 5.15)

Six mobility aids (splints or frames) were requested by the specialist physiotherapist carrying out an MS physiotherapy trial at the same time as the audit. Supply ranged from the same day to 14 days.

Table 5.15. Mobility aids supplied during the research physiotherapy trial.

Type of equipment	Department	Waiting time
Leg braces	PT trial	14 days
Bilateral ankle supports	PT trial	14 days
One multifit AFO (off the shelf)	PT trial	1 week
Pair of orthosport trainers	PT trial,NOC	1 week
Medial-arch supports (unwanted pair found)	PT trial,NOC	same day
Zimmer frame organised from SS Abingdon	PT trial, SS	2 days

AFO = ankle foot orthosis (foot drop splint); NOC = Nuffield Orthopaedic Centre; PT = physiotherapist; SS = social services.

Problems with the referral process

5.49 Referrals were made to various health professionals and departments (NHS or social services). The audit revealed 19 problems identified by 17 people (7.5%). No specific patterns to problems in individual services or departments were noted from analysis of the data, although four problems were with the Oxfordshire Wheelchair Service. These were mainly due to financial constraints imposed on the department at the time of the audit. The common themes evident were 10 cases of slow referral or slow response to a referral. There were two inappropriate referrals, one failure to refer, and one case of an extended waiting time to see a surgical consultant in a clinic at the John Radcliffe Hospital.

Problems with social security and social services

5.50 Twelve problems with social security and social services were identified during the audit by nine people (4%); these were related to financial matters (5), equipment supply (4) and care packages (3).

Department of Social Security (finances)

5.51 Five problems were related to the processing of a request for an allowance or funding:

i, ii Two problems took six months to be approved.

iii One request was delayed when the application form (which took three hours to complete) was mislaid at the office to which it was sent.

iv After a questionnaire from the DSS for reassessment for Disability Living Allowance was sent back completed, a phone call was received requesting clarification on some answers (no name was given). The person concerned became worried and phoned the DSS to confirm whether this was the correct procedure – to be told that it was not. No one could be found who would admit to having made the phone call.

v A request was made for a widow's pension, based on notification by mail from social services informing the lady concerned that she was now entitled to this following the death of her husband. Unfortunately, she was not informed that, should she take up the option of the widow's pension, her incapacity benefit would be substantially reduced and the widow's benefit taxed. This would have led to her being financially worse off.

Social Services (equipment)

5.52 Four instances were related to equipment supply:

i A piece of equipment was recommended on assessment, but social services refused to fund it.

ii A request was made for hand controls/adaptations in the person's car. This person was told that new clients go on a waiting list for one year, quotes are then obtained for conversion of the car, and the lowest quote taken. The individual concerned felt the need was immediate, otherwise it would not be possible to drive, so chose to pay for the conversion. There was some financial difficulty as a result.

iii A request for a ceiling hoist took three months to be approved because a second estimate of cost was requested. Delivery and installation of the hoist was then further delayed due to a waiting list for hoists in the area. At the six-month mark, which was the end of the audit, the hoist had still not been supplied. The case was felt to be extreme due to this person's particular problems involving two falls during transfer to a wheelchair which necessitated calling the ambulance service to help them get off the floor. Minimal contact was made by social services with the individual concerned during this period to explain the delay.

iv The last case was far more extreme due to the nature of costs involved. A request was made to the social services OT for a stair hoist in 1995. While the initial request and installation of aids were made prior to the audit period, subsequent contacts with social service during the audit period have been recorded. On assessment, the community OT decided that further aids and conversions were necessary in the home, based on the assumption that the person concerned would not be able properly to transfer in and out of a wheelchair in three years' time. At the time of the assessment, the person was walking short distances and transferring independently. The total costs of the aids and conversion of the house reached £26,000. (*Note*: there was no clinical reason to make this assumption, which was made without reference to any specialist.)

Care packages

5.53   The final three problems relate to home care packages:

i   A care package was reassessed with a view to reducing the number of hours' care supplied, but remained unchanged.

ii   The care package, which was again reassessed, was being managed under a brokerage scheme (in which the person was sharing costs for care) and was much more complex. Reduction in care hours was sought based, first, on the person concerned having more than £16,000 in the bank and, secondly, on an assumption that placement in a nursing home would be less costly, despite this person owning the home which had been designed by the architect to fit requirements. Assistance was enlisted from the community care rights project of the Oxfordshire Community Care Advisory Group to submit a waiver on psychological grounds. This was accepted, and the care package remained unchanged after considerable time spent on negotiation and emotional trauma to the person.

iii   Complications were experienced by carers involved in a home care package. They complained of hurting their backs, and were finally replaced by carers from another organisation. The original carers in this case were often different on each visit, leading to poor continuity in learning how to move the person involved.

Problems with investigations and/or treatment

5.54   During the audit, eight major tests were reported for which the person concerned had to travel to another department or hospital. (This does not include routine urine or blood tests, with which no complaints or problems were reported.) In all cases, the waiting time for an appointment was well within the limits stipulated by the Patient's Charter and were not considered a problem. Where problems were experienced, they tended to be due to the amount of time required for the relevant health professional to receive the results of the tests.

Magnetic resonance imaging

5.55 Magnetic resonance imaging (MRI) was performed in four cases. In only one case was the result received by the person concerned in under two weeks, the others taking seven, eight and 16 weeks. In two cases, it took the stated length of time to have the results sent to the appropriate health professional. In another case, the person concerned phoned after two months to find out what was happening, to be asked why they had not turned up for their appointment. It transpired that the follow-up appointment had been lost in the post. Another appointment was made for the person to receive the results.

X-rays

5.56 Three X-rays were performed, two on the same person on separate occasions at the accident and emergency department. Results were received immediately. The third was a routine request and results were received within four days.

Colonoscopy

5.57 One colonoscopy was performed, with a waiting time for results of 10 weeks.

Steroid treatment

5.58 Nine people (4%) required steroids during the audit. One of them was taking a low dose of oral steroids continuously, and it was discovered that the drug should have been stopped some months earlier. Of the remaining eight people, six required intravenous steroid treatment necessitating a period in hospital. One of them also received a follow-up intramuscular injection. Two people had an oral course of steroids lasting a number of days, managed by their GP. No specific problems were identified.

Summary

5.59 The results of the prospective audit of service use by 226 patients with MS reveal the extraordinarily wide range of presenting problems that services need to address, together with the wide range both of services involved and of specific interventions. The individual patient experiences also illustrate that some decisions are made in the absence of adequate expertise and knowledge, and that there are faults. For example, three patients developed pressure sores during hospital admission - an unacceptably high rate, given that this was only a small sample of all disabled patients admitted during the 10 months. (There is a more detailed discussion about pressure sores and other problems in Chapter 8.)

6 Results: the process of diagnosis

6.1　One of the recurring themes from patient interviews in the preliminary studies was an abiding dissatisfaction with the way the diagnosis of multiple sclerosis (MS) was communicated. There were many possible explanations for this, but the strength of this feeling made it imperative that we studied the process of diagnosis.

Method

6.2　Twenty-one people were identified as having been formally diagnosed with MS after January 1994, of whom 15 consented to an interview about the process of diagnosis. Three people recruited also participated in the first part of the audit. The age range of those interviewed was 23–58 years of age, 13 of them were women and two men. The semi-structured interview was designed to ask participants to answer 18 questions to provide a clear picture of the process of diagnosis in Oxfordshire and to identify any problems (Table 6.1). The resulting data were subjected to content analysis to identify common themes for problems occurring. It must be stressed that all the data presented below came directly from patients. No attempt was made to verify any statements. It is obviously possible that the data are affected by both faulty memory and bias.

Table 6.1. Semi-structured interview schedule for people newly diagnosed with MS.

1	When did you first experience symptoms that worried you?
2	What were those symptoms?
3	When did you seek advice regarding those symptoms?
4	Who did you seek advice from?
5	What did they suggest?
6	Did you see a consultant neurologist?
7	(If seen by a neurologist) what tests were performed by the neurologist?
8	How long did you have to wait to receive the results of the tests?
9	Who explained the results of the tests to you?
10	Who was present when the tests were explained?
11	Who told you that you had (probable) MS? ('probable' to be used for people who do not yet have a definite diagnosis)
12	Where were you told?
13	How were you told that you had MS?
14	Was any information offered?
15	Were you asked if you would like to see the MS specialist nurse?
16	Were you offered a follow-up appointment after being told you had (probable) MS?
17	Is there anything that could be done to improve how people are told that they have MS?
18	Were you asked to bring someone with you when you were told you had MS?

Semi-structured interview schedule for people newly diagnosed with multiple sclerosis

1. When did you first experience symptoms that worried you?

This question was asked to determine how quickly people were formally diagnosed from the onset of first worrying symptom(s). One person was not sure because of a lifelong history of vague symptoms. In the others, formal diagnosis was made within:

- five months of first symptoms (3);
- one year (6–12 months) (2);
- two years (5) (one of this group was not formally told their diagnosis, but the possibility was mentioned);
- 10 years (2); and
- 20 years (2).

2. What were those symptoms?

A number of first worrying symptoms were experienced by those interviewed which led to the person seeking medical advice. Ten people experienced altered sensation (ie numbness in one or more areas of the body, pins and needles), one of whom also experienced bad headaches. Two experienced light-headedness with some visual impairment, one had a limb going cold, one experienced pain down one side of the body, and one suffered urinary incontinence.

3. When did you seek advice regarding those symptoms?

Nine people sought advice within five days of experiencing worrying symptoms, two waited until they experienced the symptoms for more than five days, and four were not sure how long they waited before seeking advice.

4. Who did you seek advice from?

In all 15 cases, first advice regarding the symptoms being experienced was from their general practitioner (GP).

5. What did they suggest?

The response from GPs (ie what they suggested when advice for symptoms was sought) was mixed. In 10 cases, GPs were immediately suspicious and referred the person to a neurologist for examination within two visits (two of these people had an immediate admission to hospital due to the seriousness of the symptoms). In two cases, preliminary X-rays gave a negative result and there was immediate referral to a neurologist. In one case the GP ordered various tests, mainly for a trapped nerve. Physiotherapy was ordered and a final referral to a neurologist was not made for 10 years. In one case in which the first diagnosis was possible carpal tunnel syndrome, the person was referred to the Radcliffe Infirmary for investigation and active physiotherapy. Nerve conduction tests were inconclusive. Referral was made after the person returned to their GP with persistent symptoms. The final case was more complex. Numerous investigations in 1994 showed little, and the GP suggested a psychiatric referral. This was refused by the person concerned. In 1995, further symptoms arose leading the GP to suggest the flu, despite the person displaying paralysis down one side of the body and slurred speech. The person was finally admitted for investigation of a possible stroke the next day.

6. Did you see a consultant neurologist?

On their first visit to the Radcliffe Infirmary to see a neurologist (whether admitted or not) nine saw a consultant neurologist, although one person went as a private patient to ensure seeing someone while the symptoms persisted. Two people were not sure whether or not the person they saw was a consultant neurologist, and four people did not see one.

7. (If seen by neurologist) what tests were performed by the neurologist?

As a result of the initial visit to a neurologist, magnetic resonance imaging (MRI) was performed on 11 people, lumbar puncture on seven and EEG on three (one series of tests was not ordered by the neurologist but by an orthopaedic consultant). All 15 people remembered having blood tests at various points, but were unsure why. Visual evoked potentials were performed on three people. Eight people could not remember all the tests performed on them during this period, though MRI, lumbar puncture and EEG appeared to be the most memorable experiences.

8. How long did you have to wait to receive the results of the tests?

Six people had the results of their initial tests within two weeks, four were told within four weeks (one of these could not remember the exact time, but was sure it was within one month), one person was given the results within eight weeks, and one within ten weeks. Two people had to wait six months for their results, one due to change of address (not having notified the Radcliffe Infirmary). The second person had to wait up to six months to have all the tests completed at the Nuffield Orthopaedic Centre (a six-month wait for a nerve conduction test). One person was not given the results of her initial tests. A letter was sent to the GP, but it contained no specific results.

9. Who explained the results of the tests to you?

Eight people stated that the consultant had explained the results to them, three people had the results explained by a doctor under the neurologist, in two cases it was their GP, and in one the MS specialist nurse. One person did not have the results explained.

10. Who was present when the tests were explained?

In 10 cases only the person concerned and the person explaining the results of the tests were present when the tests were explained. In four cases, the spouse was also present, in two of which students were also present (although permission was sought in only one case). In the case in which the tests were not explained (see above) only the person and the neurologist were present during the follow-up visit.

11. Who told you that you had (probable) MS?

In 11 cases the consultant neurologist told the person concerned that they had MS or probable MS. In two cases, the GP told them the diagnosis, one of which was quickly followed up by a visit to the neurologist. The MS specialist nurse explained the diagnosis to one person, and in one case the diagnosis was not officially stated although the GP was most helpful in explaining the possibility of probable MS.

12. Where were you told?

Nine people were told in the outpatient clinic, and one was seen in the outpatient clinic but a specific diagnosis was not actually given at that time. Two people were told at their GP practice, three while inpatients (two in a side room off the ward and one during the ward round).

13. How were you told that you had MS?

Nine people were told directly by the consultant that they had MS. When one person told the consultant that she was six weeks pregnant, he was reported to have suggested a termination because she would have problems coping. The impact of being given a diagnosis of MS in this way contributed to a premature termination of the pregnancy (against her GP's advice) and a period of separation for this lady and her partner. In another case, the consultant seemed reluctant to state the words 'multiple sclerosis', and it was not until the person concerned pressed for an answer, saying that he must have some idea, that the consultant stated 'you have one of the forms of MS'. One person was told that she had lots of demyelination in her MRI scan and asked if she knew what that meant. Another was told on a preliminary visit that the symptoms were like those of MS, but the consultant did not directly state that he thought it was MS. It was not until a subsequent visit, when the consultant said that she could see the MS specialist nurse, that she finally realised the diagnosis.

Two people were told by their GPs who said that the results indicated MS. One of these described the manner in which it was done as being 'told something like she had the flu'. One person was told by the MS specialist nurse, who explained the test results and directly told the person concerned that the diagnosis was MS. Further support and information was given. One case remained unconfirmed, although a registrar on the first visit mentioned the possibility of MS. On the follow-up visit, the consultant stated that the tests were inconclusive, but wrote a letter to the GP saying that he thought it was the early stages of MS. He also said in the letter that he felt the person concerned and their spouse were over informed about MS (but he was unaware of the registrar's earlier comments). The letter was shown to the person concerned by the GP.

14. Was any information offered?

Five people interviewed were offered no information about MS when they were told their diagnosis, although one of them did not get a confirmed diagnosis of MS and another (an inpatient) actively sought advice from ward staff after receiving the news from the consultant. Three people were only given advice to contact the MS Society in Oxfordshire. One of these was also told of the possibility of treatment being given should the condition flare up again, the nature of which was not explained. Another person was also told about the MS specialist nurse (but only given her phone number).

Five other people were told about the MS specialist nurse. Two people in this group saw her directly after the clinic when they were told the diagnosis, one was given her phone number and told to ring her, and two had an appointment arranged for them by the ward staff after having been told the diagnosis (one person was also given leaflets on MS).

One person was asked by the consultant what kind of information they would like, but they had already sought out information because of their own suspicions. This person was also told about the MS specialist nurse and had an appointment arranged to see her. One person received information about MS and the MS Society and was given leaflets. This was followed up by information sessions with the GP, but neither the neurologist nor the GP informed the person about the MS specialist nurse.

15. Were you asked if you would like to see the MS specialist nurse?

Although an MS specialist nurse was employed by the department of neurology at the time these 15 patients were given their diagnosis, only 10 of them were informed that they could see her if desired. They found out about her in varying ways. Six people were told at the time of diagnosis by the neurologist (although one had to wait almost four months to see her). One person was told by a nurse comforting them directly after being told the diagnosis; two found out (from staff) as inpatients on a ward at the Radcliffe Infirmary, and the MS specialist nurse introduced herself to one person on admission three weeks after diagnosis. Five people were not told about the MS specialist nurse during the process of being diagnosed, although they may have had contact with her subsequently as a result of MS open days held in Oxfordshire.

16. Were you offered a follow-up appointment after being told you had (probable) MS?

Two people accepted the offer of a follow-up visit at the Radcliffe Infirmary; one of these was seen by a registrar on the follow-up visit, not by the consultant. One person was given the choice of a follow-up appointment with the neurologist or the GP, and chose the GP. Ten people were not offered a follow-up appointment at the Radcliffe Infirmary, although two were told to return to their GP if they experienced any further problems or had any queries and that the GP could refer them back at any time. One person was offered follow-up visits with the GP but not at the Radcliffe Infirmary. Another person was referred to Rivermead Rehabilitation Centre, and followed-up by the MS specialist nurse in due course. Another person had an admission organised as a result of the diagnosis, so a follow-up visit was not deemed necessary, and one person was followed-up routinely post-discharge as an inpatient.

17. Is there anything that could be done to improve how people are told that they have MS?

Seven people would have preferred to have been told their diagnosis in a better manner. Two people did not like the way they were told, and six described the process as 'vague', 'hazy' or 'very off-hand'. One person would have liked the neurologist to have explained things more clearly. Six of the 15 people interviewed commented on the neurologist's behaviour as ranging from 'off-hand' to 'being made to feel like they were wasting the neurologist's time'. Seven people would have liked more factual information about MS, including more reading material, and a better attitude to giving information. One person felt more follow-up was needed. Two people would have liked more emotional support from the time of diagnosis. Two people had no complaints about the way the diagnosis was delivered, although one of them wanted more information. One person would have liked more understanding from their GP, and one also commented that it would have been preferable to have had the MS specialist nurse available at the time of being told the diagnosis instead of later.

18. Were you asked to bring someone with you when you were told you had MS?

Thirteen of those interviewed had not been told to bring someone with them when the diagnosis was given; four of this group brought their spouse anyway, but one spouse was left in the waiting room rather than being invited to accompany their partner into the clinic. One person was in hospital when told the diagnosis, but no attempt had been made to have any family present. One person was also told the diagnosis in hospital, and the husband was present – but this was coincidental rather than planned.

Summary

6.3   The interviews suggest that the process of diagnosis itself was usually reasonably quick. The main criticisms related to the way in which it was told to patients and to the follow-up arrangements after the diagnosis was made.

7 | Results: interventions by the audit researchers

7.1   The initial plan had been to collect data on service process from service providers and to compare performance against agreed standards. However, when the audit/researchers moved on to collecting data from individual patients it was inevitable that they would become much more involved in patient affairs on a day-to-day basis. It was not practical, and would often have been unethical, to ignore difficulties that patients discussed with the auditor. It was therefore decided that the audit would capitalise on the active involvement of the auditor. We reasoned that patients would approach the auditor only when, or if, the service already involved was failing to resolve matters satisfactorily (in the eyes of the patients). This situation could be considered evidence.

Results

7.2   There were 32 occasions involving 25 people (11%) during the audit when the researcher felt compelled to intervene. Two of these arose when people phoned the researcher to request specific information unrelated to the audit but about multiple sclerosis (MS), and the researcher felt it appropriate to supply the information (or where to get it). Twenty-seven interventions were more serious in nature, and specific advice was given with special reference as to whom to contact to hasten a solution to a problem causing distress or unnecessary suffering. Six of these were advice to have their general practitioner (GP) refer them to the consultant in neurological disability. In six cases, the researcher felt the situation was so serious that contact was made either by phone or letter to the health professional concerned to inform them of the situation or to state concerns about what was going on. In one case, the person concerned was encouraged to write a letter of complaint; in another, because of stresses on the family, the person was encouraged to write a letter to a health professional to hasten an appointment.

7.3   The types of problems experienced varied:

   ▪ medical problems (17): seven of these were urinary problems, and one a cognitive problem with which the family was struggling to cope;

   ▪ problems with equipment supply (4);

   ▪ social problems, such as the need for emergency day care (3);

   ▪ a problem with the DHSS (1);

   ▪ a prescribed drug that had not been stopped when it should have been (1);

   ▪ referral to community physiotherapy after surgery (1).

Summary

7.4   These results show that services quite frequently fall at least below the standards expected by the patients.

8 Critical review of the study

8.1 This two-year project demonstrated that an audit specifically investigating all (health) services delivered to patients with multiple sclerosis (MS) could not realistically be undertaken in the traditional way because of the complexity both of the clinical problems faced by patients and of the organisation of service delivery. It has, however, generated a wealth of data which may help focus future attempts to audit similar services, and has allowed the development of a method for monitoring services. The project itself probably improved services through raising awareness and allowing the development of easily accessible expert advice from one person (the audit researcher).

8.2 Even if it had been possible to assess services against standards, a full audit cycle would not have been possible for many reasons. Perhaps the most important was the continuing changes already underway in response to local and national initiatives, which meant that services were never stable. In addition, the project inevitably led to changes in service profile and provision, and research projects provided additional input which again altered service delivery.

8.3 The two outstanding messages from this study are:

i Patients with MS have extremely complex problems, with multiple impairments and disabilities superimposed upon varied social circumstances.

ii They are faced with a complex patchwork of services, all of which focus on a particular *intervention* but none of which focuses on MS.

8.4 The implications of these messages for people developing services will be discussed in Chapter 9. This chapter will concentrate upon a discussion of some specific areas:

i Drawing valid conclusions: weaknesses in the study.

ii Clinical issues.

iii Other issues.

iv Audit in a rapidly changing environment.

v Complexity of illness and services.

Drawing valid conclusions: weaknesses in the study

8.5 Before other services contemplate changing their services or undertaking an audit on the basis of this study it must be considered whether circumstances surrounding this audit were so unusual as to compromise the study's validity, and whether the methods were too weak to allow any conclusions to be drawn.

8.6 Oxfordshire Health Authority covers a mixed urban and rural area with a population of about 560,000. The neurology services have had a long-standing interest in MS, mostly related to pharmacological treatments, and Oxfordshire also has relatively well developed specialist disability services. These factors might be expected to make services for this group of patients better than average, but should not otherwise reduce their general applicability.

8.7 The methods used have some obvious weaknesses:

    i   The sample was selected, and not necessarily representative of all patients. However, the volunteers might, if anything, have been more articulate and more aware of how to obtain services rather than the reverse.

    ii   Patients with severe disability were probably under-represented because they would be less able to participate.

    iii The data collected in the audit of prevalent cases were checked to an extent, but some contacts were probably missed. The details relating to the contacts that were made were verified.

    iv The data relating to the process of diagnosis are obviously subject to great bias. Information was obtained only from patients and after some months had elapsed. Nevertheless, the results do represent the *patient's perception of and satisfaction with the process*, which is perhaps the important aspect on which to focus.

8.8 We believe that the findings in this study are sufficiently robust to be used more widely. The precise percentages may be in slight error and some areas of concern may have been missed, but the broad messages seem consistent.

Clinical issues

Urinary problems

8.9 The most common single symptom area was urinary control, with 78 occurrences in 39 people, 18 of them experiencing more than one occurrence, and six of those 18 people experiencing three or more episodes during the 10-month audit. All patients saw their general practitioner (GP), and 20 were also seen by other specialists: six were referred to a urologist and 14 saw nurses. However, 19 people saw only their GP and were not referred on to services that specifically deal with urological problems. Eight of those 19 experienced more than one occurrence of a urinary problem, and one had experienced three episodes of bladder disturbance. These observations raise one question, which cannot be answered: are GPs managing patients with urinary tract symptoms effectively and efficiently, or should patients be referred more frequently and/or earlier to other specialists?

Mobility

8.10 In terms of number of reports, the second most common symptom or problem concerned mobility: 64 problems reported by 58 people. Fewer mobility problems were reported than urinary problems, but more people experienced them. Of these 58 people, 28 were treated by a hospital or community physiotherapist at some point during the audit, whereas 30 people were not so referred despite new MS symptoms or problems arising. One person in fact had 'corns on the feet', a podiatry problem not a physiotherapy problem, so 29 people could possibly have benefited from seeing a physiotherapist. The data do not allow any firm conclusions at present because:

    ▓   there is little evidence that physiotherapy necessarily benefits patients,[23,24] and

    ▓   the decision not to refer might have been appropriate in each instance, although it is equally possible that all 29 people would have benefited.

Neurogenic pain

8.11   Complex neurogenic pain (three with trigeminal neuralgia), which is often difficult to treat, was suffered by 13 people. None of these patients were referred to a neurologist at the Radcliffe Infirmary, although one person was referred to the maxillofacial surgery and orthodontics department in Oxford and three were referred to the consultant in neurological disability. Only one person was referred to the local specialist pain clinic during the audit period, despite the clinic's ability to offer assistance in this area. Nine people were treated for the problem by their GP. The success of the various treatments was difficult to determine as many people continued to experience pain beyond the end of the audit. These observations raise questions about the recognition and management of neurogenic pain by non-experts.

Pressure areas

8.12   There were 14 pressure areas, three contracted while in hospital during the audit period, two serious enough to require consultation with a plastic surgeon (one in a community hospital, the other in the acute hospital). While relatively few in number, any serious pressure sores should always be a matter of concern. Since only a relatively small proportion of all the disabled people in hospital was studied over a relatively short time, the implication is that many people develop pressure sores in hospital.

General deterioration

8.13   More than 40 episodes of 'general deterioration' were reported by 30 people. It is difficult to evaluate what this means as reported by patients. Only 11 people saw a specialist: five were seen by a neurologist at the Radcliffe Infirmary, another five were assessed by the consultant in neurological disability, and one person saw both.

Other issues

Information and advice

8.14   Twenty-five people sought information or advice about MS on 49 occasions (not including the 14 times the MS specialist nurse at the Radcliffe Infirmary was contacted for advice). In most of these cases advice was sought from the GP. At present, most people obtain advice from professionals who may not have specialist knowledge and/or the information needed.

Newly diagnosed patients

8.15   It is difficult to interpret the audit of newly diagnosed patients, but it was clear that many patients were not satisfied with the process. Their dissatisfaction was not with those aspects of the service that form the focus of government concern (eg waiting times) but with the attitudes of clinicians and the time allocated to follow-up. It is unfortunately true that in a pressurised service with long waiting lists for diagnosis clinicians may not have the apparent luxury of time for giving information and support. It was disappointing that the specialist nurse did not seem to be well used.

Seeking help

8.16 Comparison between the prevalence of symptoms giving problems all the time prior to the study and the frequency of problems/symptoms presented to health professionals during the audit demonstrates that, in general, people suffering symptoms of MS do not always seek help (two examples being problems with fatigue and sensation). The reasons are unclear, but general impressions from the audit suggest that people may either perhaps not recognise that something can be done to help their problem or have sought help in the past and few solutions have been suggested.

Conclusions

8.17 In the absence of definitive evidence on the benefit of many of the potential interventions, and in the absence of detailed clinical information on each patient, it is difficult to draw firm conclusions. However, it is of some concern that three patients developed pressure sores within a 10-month period, and that many patients with neurogenic pain were not referred to specialist services despite failure to control their pain. There is accumulating evidence that a specialist multiprofessional disability service can benefit patients,[25,26] so the failure to refer patients with new problems is thus also of some concern.

Audit in a changing environment

8.18 The clinical audit process is based on the assumption that the service being audited is relatively stable, with no major changes occurring. Although this seemed to be the situation when the project started, many factors outside our control caused services to change quite dramatically during the project.

The effect of the audit project

8.19 The project itself naturally drew attention to services related to patients with MS. This was inevitable, because we consulted widely with all actual and potential service providers and purchasers at all levels. This might alone have modified services, knowing that we would be investigating the performance of each service.

Beta-interferon

8.20 Beta-interferon was licensed, and Oxfordshire chose to spend most of the £300,000 allocated for this drug on improving general services. In practice, most money was used to fund a consultant neurologist interested in pharmacological treatments and urological problems, and a specialist nurse. This may have changed the service, especially relating to diagnosis, counselling and bladder management. These are all areas identified as causing great concern in the initial investigations. To an extent, the very fact of asking about service deficiencies led to a direct response.

The local branch of the MS Society

8.21 Coincident with the start of this project, the local branch of the MS Society acquired a new chairman who initiated many new services, both those delivered by the MS Society and those delivered by the health services (through her contacts within the health authority purchasing department). The branch started a successful open day once a month, which was attended by at least 60 people, when patients could directly access local disability services. This arose after the initial survey had revealed such a high level of dissatisfaction with disability services.

Review of disability services

8.22 Lastly, Oxfordshire conducted an extensive review of services for physically disabled people during the project, with widespread consultation. This again led to significant service developments, such as the establishment of a day centre and an out-reach service in Witney (a local town).

Complexity of illness and services

8.23 The enormous variety of problems faced by patients is evident from the data collected concerning both prevalent and incident problems. The variety of services dispersed through many organisations, locations and professions is also evident. This interaction between complex patient problems and complex services makes it impossible to undertake any systematic audit of services for patients with MS. It probably also makes it difficult for the patient.

8.24 The only person seen by the patients with any frequency was their GP. However, MS is a rare condition for GPs who are unlikely to be familiar with managing most of the problems. Furthermore, they are likely to be daunted by the complexity of services for patients with MS, not knowing to whom they should refer the patient.

8.25 Two particular observations in this audit are notable and suggest that people perceive the need for some single specialist 'point of reference' when seeking help for patients with MS:

i   The audit investigator became involved in the management of a significant number of people (and many more telephoned for help).

ii The commonest single specialist consultation was with a doctor with a special interest in neurological disability.

Summary

8.26 Various areas of great concern were highlighted within the first few months of the audit, which coincided with – and may have precipitated – some changes that significantly altered the services. Although it might be claimed that these changes were a result of the audit project, they cannot be counted as a success for audit itself as changes occurred before any standards had been set and performance documented. Given the increasing frequency of short-term special initiatives emanating from central government, it is likely that similar problems will face any future audits covering a wide range of services. A better method of quality control and improvements than the traditional approach to audit is needed.

Part 3
Application of the audit results to other diseases causing chronic disability

9 Planning a service for patients with chronic disability: recommendations

Features of multiple sclerosis of wider applicability

9.1 The study reported in the previous chapters focused on one specific group of patients identified by a particular disease diagnosis. A number of characteristics of multiple sclerosis (MS) may also apply to other chronic medical conditions, and it is likely that the findings of the audit will have much wider relevance. These features include:

 i MS is often a difficult diagnosis for the primary care doctor or district general hospital (DGH) general physician to make, and frequently requires access to specialist advice in a tertiary centre.

 ii Problems associated with MS are difficult for doctors in a DGH to manage. Few develop specific expertise in the management of MS, partly because they concentrate their expertise in other areas of medicine and partly because there are relatively few cases of MS in each district.

 iii Patients with MS experience significant disability at a relatively young age, with significant psychological and social consequences, but they live an almost normal lifespan.

 iv The rehabilitation and support services normally available locally usually focus on helping older people and will rarely have specific expertise in MS.

 v At the same time, many in the NHS regard local services such as physiotherapy or occupational therapy as generic services able to respond to any disability, without recognising that specific issues for MS are quite different from the problems of, for example, ageing.

 vi There are no formal, disease-specific schemes for the co-ordination of diagnosis, treatment, management or support of patients with MS. Health services are planned at district level, yet most clinical expertise in MS is available only at regional tertiary centres.

9.2 These general features clearly apply to other neurological conditions such as the muscular dystrophies or motor neuron disease, and will also be relevant to other relatively rare conditions affecting other organs.

9.3 The situation is different for other, much more common, chronic disorders such as diabetes, chronic obstructive airways disease or rheumatoid arthritis for which there are specialist physicians and support staff in most DGHs and often disease-specific liaison staff working within the community.

9.4 The lessons learned from this audit are likely to be relevant to a much wider population with chronic disease and long-term disability. In particular, there may be scope for combining the organisation of services for MS with those for other neurological disabling conditions (possibly even including patients with learning disabilities) that share the need to access the NHS at local, district and tertiary levels. This study might help in two ways:

i   An attempt was made to monitor the quality of the totality of NHS care delivered to one group of patients who at various times used almost all types of services. Most audit is top down, focusing on a particular service in isolation (eg physiotherapy provision as it applies to all patients), whereas our approach began with the patient and their requirements without any preconceptions of what the service should be. This approach, in effect a 'needs assessment', is likely to be relevant to others who wish to audit services from the patient's perspective.

ii This study illustrates some of the problems that any ideal service should overcome, and thus may be helpful in planning services more generally.

9.5   This chapter discusses how to monitor the quality of a patchwork of services delivered to one group of patients, and how to improve services for patients with MS. It suggests that a specialist neurological disability service, closely allied to acute neurological and neurosurgical services, and linking closely with social services and other 'generic' services (eg wheelchair services) would be the most efficient and effective way to offer services to patients with MS and other disabling neurological diseases. Properly set up, it is likely to be able to provide a better quality of care that will be perceived as more useful and relevant by patients. It may not necessarily be more costly than the present unco-ordinated situation, but this study did not consider the cost implications and further work on the relative cost efficacy is needed. However, there can be little argument that the present situation needs to be improved.

9.6   Similar specialist disability services may be needed for other diseases such as cardiopulmonary and rheumatological disorders, allied to the acute medical services and linked into generic services. Their organisation is, however, likely to be different because of the increased availability of expert services at district level and because of the increased opportunity for primary care to develop expertise because these conditions and the problems they pose are much more common.

Monitoring service quality: problems in data collection

9.7   The audit proved quite successful at obtaining data, but there were a number of difficulties for which we make the following recommendations:

▷ **Recommendations:**

i   A 10-month study period to complete the audit was too long to sustain the interest of many people. Six months would be more likely to sustain the interest of the participants, and more manageable for a researcher in terms of data collection.

ii Despite the slow start to the audit, 226 people with MS produced far too much data and far too many contacts for one researcher to keep contact with. The experience of this study suggests that perhaps 150 people with MS would provide the right balance between keeping the workload manageable and ensuring complete and accurate data. Different numbers might be needed with different diseases or services.

iii The audit card was a good way to validate contacts but, where possible, prospective telephone contact should be maintained with each patient, and contacts with health professionals be confirmed to maintain accuracy. Contacts recorded and validated by general practitioners (GPs) in Oxfordshire were the most successful, but those with other professionals working in the community were more difficult.

iv If such an audit is undertaken in the future, an additional six months should be allowed for analysis and writing up of the report as the data collected can be large and cumbersome. This would make the total time required about 18 months: six months each for preparation, data collection and analysis. The time taken for feedback and instituting change is difficult to predict.

v Many health professionals, especially GPs, now require a signed consent form from a patient before they will release any information. This proved quite a problem in the later stages of the audit. Some GPs were happy with a photocopy of a consent form, but a number requested an original. To prevent any future problems, either a copy or a second original should be supplied to the GP prior to commencing data collection. While time-consuming, this one action should save considerable time in the long run.

vi Traditionally in audit, the research is initiated and undertaken by one service provider, ensuring some commitment to taking action to improve service quality. This approach is difficult to pursue when studying all services delivered from a range of different providers to a specific group of patients because individual service providers will rarely see such a global audit as being relevant. Consequently, they will not necessarily be committed to undertaking any necessary remedial action. We would therefore suggest that this type of audit needs to be instigated by the service commissioners responsible for ensuring that the needs of the whole population are met. Given that services span at least health, social services and housing (and possibly employment and education), it is important that all major organisations are involved, not just health.

9.8 With these relatively straightforward precautions, we believe that audit of services to consider all the needs of specified groups of patients can be undertaken successfully.

Improving service delivery for multiple sclerosis

9.9 The results of our audit suggest that services for people with MS in Oxfordshire, and possibly elsewhere, could be greatly improved in a number of areas.

Knowledge about multiple sclerosis among health professionals

9.10 A consistent comment from patients was that most health and social service professionals had limited knowledge of MS because many of them have only infrequent contact with people with MS. Our study confirmed that some NHS professionals appeared to be either unaware of their ignorance or had untrue beliefs about MS. Consequently, patients with MS tend to believe they know more about MS than their advisors.

Dealing with problems

9.11 The findings in the audit also highlight how little patients know about symptom management in MS and how to deal with various problems that arise. It is therefore unwise to assume that patients can succeed at being their own advocates. In many neurological conditions, memory, concentration and other cognitive capacities that underlie successful self-advocacy are themselves affected. Self-advocacy also requires the patient to be fully informed about all potential problems and about the possible solutions, and to have sufficient self-confidence to undertake the task. While obviously some patients with some conditions can be successful at self-advocacy, it is not a policy that can be applied to the majority.

> **Recommendation:**

We would suggest that any patient with MS who develops a troublesome new problem should be considered for assessment by an expert multidisciplinary team. In this way, the nature of the problem can be established and an informed plan of management instigated. Often the interventions themselves can be undertaken by other people. The team is needed simply to ensure an appropriate level of intervention.

Referrals to appropriate services: multidisciplinary services

9.12 The other obvious finding is that patients with MS may be seen almost anywhere within health and social services, and multiple referrals are both common and necessary. However, the audit revealed the frequent failure to utilise existing services (eg pain clinic, MS specialist nurse) for the complex problems that arise in MS. It is not realistic to expect services within each specialist domain (eg urology, cardiology, rheumatology) to have a specific subservice for patients with MS. Specialist services need to specialise in their own areas of expertise across many diseases, but it may be practical for specific individuals within the service to take responsibility for specified chronic conditions or groups of conditions. However organised, the NHS systems need to improve ease of access for such patients, and primary and non-specialist clinicians need to know who to refer, where, how and when. This implies the need for a local policy so that all concerned know who is responsible for different aspects of care.

> **Recommendation:**

The establishment of a multidisciplinary expert team might focus expertise and act as a central 'sorting service', linking patients to other appropriate specialist or generic services.

Assessments

9.13 It was also apparent that large numbers of people are unassessed for long periods of time, leaving minor problems to progress unchecked. The result is a management model based on 'crisis management' in which only those people experiencing serious relapse or progression get reassessed to determine their needs. Those who fail to meet the serious criteria do not get thorough assessment on a regular basis, which may possibly lead to unnecessary disability.

> **Recommendation:**

While purely speculative and needing further research, there may be a role for some form of regular review, perhaps by post or telephone.

Making the diagnosis

9.14 In relation to making the diagnosis, we can only note the low level of patient satisfaction shown in the audit.

> **Recommendation:**

We recommend that neurology services consider carefully how satisfaction with the diagnosis can be improved. It should be possible to set out UK guideline criteria for how a diagnosis of MS can be confidently made. This might also include criteria for non-specialists to know who should and who should not be referred for specialist assessments.

Service design

9.15 There is slim evidence relating to best practice specifically for patients with MS. Evidence from stroke, however, strongly supports the effectiveness of specialist multidisciplinary co-ordinated services for patients with complex problems,[27] and there is some supportive evidence for MS.[25,26] It is now generally accepted that complex and rare problems are best managed by specialist services. This underlies the development of most medical specialties, and is being recognised for such conditions as breast cancer and diabetes. The important first step is to recognise and agree that troublesome disability is a complex and relatively rare problem that warrants specialist services.

9.16 The experience of this project was that the auditor herself was instrumental in improving service quality for individual patients. The major underlying fault appeared to be a lack of knowledge among 'front-line' staff, which supports the contention that disability requires expert assessment.

Model of service delivery

9.17 No one model of service delivery can be recommended on the basis of published evidence, but the model shown in Fig 9.1 would seem to be one effective way of providing patients with a central point of expert reference that requires little reorganisation of current services. This model is based loosely around the World Health Organization (WHO) ICIDH model of illness.

9.18 The diagnosis and management of any underlying pathology are the primary responsibility of the GP in the community, aided by hospital specialist services where necessary. Within hospital, most specialties are based around organs (eg cardiology, neurology) and treatment modalities (eg medicine, surgery, radiotherapy). The diagnosis and management of disability would also usually start with the GP (if the disease is not known), but may start with other community services. Any patient whose disability is persistent or troublesome, and not quickly and easily resolved, should be seen by the appropriate specialist disability service. For patients with acute severe disability, the referral is likely to come from the hospital team.

9.19 There are already several specialised disability/rehabilitation services, usually closely linked to an associated hospital specialty. Paediatric and geriatric services currently manage both the disease and the disability. The disabilities associated with cardiac, pulmonary and rheumatological diseases are different to those for conditions such as MS, and there will be little overlap between the way that services are run for them and for a neurological disability. Spinal injury already has a specialist disability service, as have amputee services (in some parts of the country at least), and stroke patients may in some areas.

Multidisciplinary team

9.20 Each specialist disability service would consist of a multidisciplinary team. This would always include a doctor trained in disability medicine (rehabilitation) appropriate to the specialist service, and most should also contain nurses, physiotherapists, occupational therapists, clinical psychologists and social workers as dedicated members (not shared) of the team. Speech and language therapists will often be vital, but not in all disability service teams. Dietitians, orthoptists etc may need to be attached to or part of the team, depending upon the

Figure 9.1 Levels of service. illustrated for neurological disability.

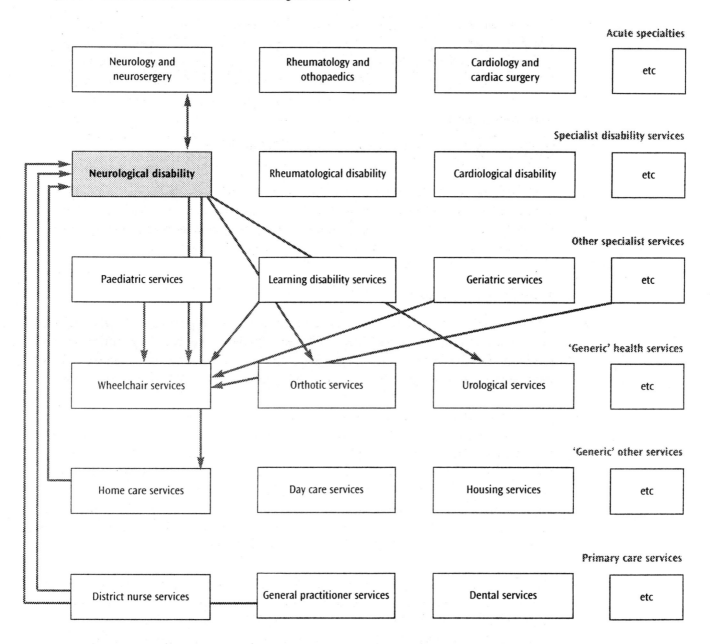

client group. As a general rule, the team should have a sufficient variety of professions to manage at least 90% of all problems that arise. All senior staff in the team should be specialised in the appropriate field.

Links to acute specialties

9.21 The specialist disability service would have close links to its acute specialties, and also act as the link to other services which are 'generic' from the point of view of the clientele. For example, the urological service would be the specialist disability service for patients with bladder diseases, but also be available to patients from any other specialist disability service. It would also link closely with other primary care community services provided by health or social services.

Generic disability services

9.22 A group of generic disability services would specialise in particular interventions (rather than in patient groups). Examples include the wheelchair and orthotics services, both of which will be used by almost all disability services. They could be considered as analogous to the pathology services in acute medical management, specialised but used by all.

Community services

9.23 Finally, the community services, which have a twofold specialism:

i   They know the local area: who does what well, which shops are accessible to the blind, where the best adult education is, etc.

ii They will get to know the patient and the family well over time. All specialist disability services will link back to community services. Patients seen by any of the community services could be referred back to the specialist disability services.

Specific recommendations for multiple sclerosis services

For patients with MS, it is recommended that each district:

- has a doctor and nurse (or other non-medical professional) with special responsibility for and expertise in the management of patients with MS;

- develops a directory of services and people with appropriate expertise for all the more common problems;

- considers developing a neurological disability service which is:
  - multidisciplinary,
  - specialist, with expertise and interest, and
  - co-ordinated;

- develops an ongoing educational programme for all professional staff who come into contact with patients with MS (including social services staff).

10 | Conclusions

i   This project has shown that it is probably not possible for an individual health authority to audit services provided to patients with multiple sclerosis (MS) in an isolated manner using traditional methods. There is no discrete MS service, and patients use a huge variety of services spanning many organisations and specialties. The project suggests that developing the role of a specialist MS person, probably a nurse (but possibly from any profession) might allow both an improvement in the service offered to patients with MS and a means of undertaking audit to ensure that quality services are maintained.

ii   The results highlight the extreme variety and complexity of the problems experienced by patients with MS. They also emphasise the complexity of current service arrangements, a complexity unlikely to be unique to Oxfordshire. Much of the complexity arises from the policy of successive governments that have separated health from social services and have also separated the budgets, all of which are cash limited.

iii   The results also seem to show that professionals need much more education about MS and disability in general, and that some professionals may need to improve their attitude to disabled patients and to patients with MS. It is unclear to what extent some problems simply arise from the great pressure now experienced by all services and by all staff in services.

iv   If some direction and organisation could be instilled into the MS services (possibly linked to the other neurological disabilities), it is likely that patients would experience a more accessible and more efficient service. Co-ordinating activity so that the right thing gets done for the right person at the right time is likely to be more cost-effective, especially if it helps to prevent chronic disability progressing because the opportunities for remedial action were missed. Patients have a right to better care than has been described in this report.

v   It is recommended that health authorities reconsider their provision of disability support for MS, and consider developing a specialist disability service either locally or in collaboration with neighbouring districts around a regional centre. There will need to be links with most of the major 'medical specialties' and for specified clinicians to be responsible for the ongoing assessment and management of the long-term disability seen in this patient group.

References

1   Rudd AG, Irwin P, Rutledge Z, Lowe D, *et al*. The national sentinel audit for stroke: a tool for raising standards of care. *J R Coll Physicians Lond* 1999;33:460–4.

2   Wade DT, de Jong B. Recent advances in rehabilitation. *Br Med J* 2000;320:1385–8.

3   Harrison J. *The young disabled adult*. London: The Royal College of Physicians, 1986.

4   Cantrell EG, Dawson J, Glastonbury G. *Prisoners of handicap*. London: Royal Association for Disability and Rehabilitation, 1985.

5   Ekdawi MY, Conning AM. *Psychiatric rehabilitation: a practical guide*. London: Chapman & Hall, 1994.

6   Brown RI, Hughson EA. *Behavioural and social rehabilitation and training*, 2nd edn. London: Chapman & Hall, 1993.

7   Post MWM, de Witte LP, Schrijvers AJP. Quality of life and the ICIDH: towards an integrated conceptual model for rehabilitation outcomes research. *Clin Rehabil* 1999;13:5–15.

8   Badley EM. An introduction to the concepts and classifications of the International Classification of Impairments, Disabilities and Handicaps. *Disabil Rehabil* 1993;15:161–78.

9   ICIDH-2: International Classification of Functioning and Disability. Beta-2 draft. Geneva: World Health Organisation, 1999. http://www.who.int/msa/mnh/ems/icidh/

10 Wood P. International Classification of Impairments, Disabilities and Handicaps: a manual of classification relating to the consequences of disease. Geneva: World Health Organization, 1980.

11 Wade DT. Personal context as a focus for rehabilitation. *Clin Rehabil* 2000;14:115–8.

12 Schwartz CE. Teaching coping skills enhances quality of life more than peer support: results of a randomized trial with multiple sclerosis patients. *Health Psychol* 1999;18:211–20.

13 Wade DT. Disability, rehabilitation and spinal injury. In: Donaghy M (ed). *Brain's diseases of the nervous system*, Ch 6. Oxford: Oxford University Press, 2001.

14 Wade DT. Evidence relating to goal planning in rehabilitation. *Clin Rehabil* 1998;12:273–5.

15 Cunningham C, Horgan F, Keane N, Connolly P, *et al*. Detection of disability by different members of an interdisciplinary team. *Clin Rehabil* 1996;10:247–54.

16 Hopkins A. *Measuring the quality of medical care*. London: The Royal College of Physicians, 1990.

17 Cairns C, Shepherd G. Pathways to the future for community diabetes care. In: Wilson J (ed). *Integrated care management: the path to success*. Oxford: Butterworth-Heinemann, 1997.

18 Wade DT, Langton Hewer R. Epidemiology of some neurological diseases with special reference to workload on the NHS. *Int Rehabil Med* 1986;8:129–37.

19 Forbes RB, Swingler RJ. Estimating the prevalence of multiple sclerosis in the United Kingdom by using capture-recapture methodology. *Am J Epidemiol* 1999;149:1016–24.

20 Wade DT. Services for patients with multiple sclerosis. *J Neurol Neurosurg Psychiatry* 1997;63:275–8.

21 Sharrack B, Hughes RAC. The Guy's Disability Scale: a new disability measure for multiple sclerosis. *Multiple Sclerosis* 1999;5:223–33.

22 Thibodeau JA, Hawkins JW. Developing an original tool for research. *Nurse Pract* 1988;13:56–9.

23 Lord SE, Wade DT, Halligan PW. A comparison of two physiotherapy treatment approaches to improve walking in multiple sclerosis: a pilot randomised controlled study. *Clin Rehabil* 1998;12:477–86.

24 Fuller KJ, Dawson K, Wiles CM. Physiotherapy in chronic multiple sclerosis: a controlled trial. *Clin Rehabil* 1996;10:195–204.

25 Freeman JA, Langdon DW, Hobart JC, Thompson AJ. The impact of inpatient rehabilitation on progressive multiple sclerosis. *Ann Neurol* 1997;42:236–44.

26 Di Fabio RP, Soderberg J, Choi T, Hansen CR, Schapiro RT. Extended outpatient rehabilitation: its influence on symptom frequency, fatigue, and functional status for persons with progressive multiple sclerosis. *Arch Phys Med Rehabil* 1998;79:141–6.

27 Stroke Unit Trialists' Collaboration. Collaborative systematic review of the randomised trials of organised inpatient (stroke unit) care after stroke. *Br Med J* 1997;314:1151–9.